KEIDRYCH RHYS
The Van Pool: Collected Poems

Keidrych Rhys, drawn by Stanley Lewis

KEIDRYCH RHYS

The Van Pool: Collected Poems

edited by Charles Mundye

Seren is the book imprint of
Poetry Wales Press Ltd.
57 Nolton Street, Bridgend, Wales, CF31 3AE

www.serenbooks.com
facebook.com/SerenBooks
Twitter: @SerenBooks

The right of Keidrych Rhys to be identified as
the author of this work has been asserted in accordance
with the Copyright, Designs and Patents Act, 1988.

ISBN 978-1-85411-582-9

A CIP record for this title is available from the British Library.

The publisher acknowledges the financial assistance of the Welsh Books Council.

Cover Image: 131169 Keidrych Rhys, photographed by Ida Kar, Llanybri,
Wales, c. 1945. Reproduced by kind permission, © National Portrait Gallery,
London

Printed in Plantin by the CPI Group (UK) Ltd, Croydon

Contents

Uncollected Poems

Unpublished Poems

List of Illustrations

Foreword

A Boxing Day baby, he was born at the farm of Llwynyrynn – the ash-grove – a cluster of green fields scumbled across the last rocky westward thrust of The Black Mountain where it falls away to Afon Tywi. Bethlehem was the nearest village, Llandeilo of the Lord Rhys and the ancient kings of Deheubarth his closest town. Everywhere around his childhood home was resonance, were reminders of written and unwritten histories: Dinefwr, Y Gaer Fawr, Tri Chrug, Carreg Cennen.

Dyffryn Ceidrych was the name of this locality, after the Nant Ceidrych that rises by the site of the Roman villa and flows round Bethlehem to mingle with the Tywi at Pengoilan. In time-honoured Welsh tradition, as a young man he took from this *bro* his bardic name, formally registering it by deed poll when he was twenty-six. Plain Ronnie Jones legally became Keidrych Rhys. There has been much discussion of why he chose not to spell this in accepted Welsh fashion, with a 'C'. Perhaps there was a deliberate harking-back to the archaic Welsh usage (as in 'Pedeir Keinc y Mabinogi'); perhaps, given the distaste with which he viewed his own alarming portrait by the painter Cedric Morris, he had no wish for confusion or mispronunciation? Whatever the reason, the *mythos* was established, and with it an abounding confidence:

> Though we write in English, we are rooted in Wales.

You can easily imagine a later and more eminent poetic Welsh Ronald making that statement. What you cannot imagine is for any other twentieth-century poet writing in English from Wales to display comparable visceral proofs of that rootedness. Like the rocks of his native *bro*, they crop up everywhere in the work of this 'victim of a widened horizon'. He drew the contrast between himself and his contemporaries sharply on this point:

> What it is to have water running near one's own house
> With eels in it – alone – real – a one-syllabled water language.
> Those town fellows have borrowed beetles in their shoes!

Terse? For sure – but how aptly it undercuts the all-too-familiar inauthentic bucolic strivings of other poets. With Keidrych, language and description are blood-simple. He clearly knows:

> Oh the young devils are tough with bleeding navels lean on
> ground;
> by elements torn, brown hairstuff licked, prayer suck, born
> worth a £.

'...in a way it was you who started it all', Glyn Jones wrote to him, as prologue to his seminal book of essays, *The Dragon has Two Tongues*.

In a way – and of course the point can be argued. What's beyond dispute is that there is significance here. *Wales* under Keidrych's long editorship was the vehicle for what we now recognize as the first great wave of consciously Anglo-Welsh literature (just as its second and consolidating phase occurred under Robin Reeves' inspired editorship of *New Welsh Review*). Vernon Watkins, Lynette Roberts, Dylan Thomas, Robert Graves, Idris Davies, R.S. Thomas – Keidrych published them all. It helped that he was, in M. Wynn Thomas's perceptive, ever-amused view, 'brash...exuberant...unabashed by self-contradiction...flamboyant...knockabout.'

His own best work is early, from the war years and before. Inspiration himself for his first wife Lynette Roberts' finest poem, the late-modernist master-work *Gods with Stainless Ears* – a poem that invites qualified comparison, though from a quite different sector of experience, with David Jones' magnificent *In Parenthesis* – by the time of the appearance of *Gods* in 1951 Keidrych's own poetry was more or less done.

I knew of him as a shadowy figure, diasporate somehow, rural Sir Gâr let loose on mid-century London, an outsider exiled from the place of his belonging – could imagine him in a corner of a Museum Street pub sharing a pint with Paddy Kavanagh – men from green deserts in a city oasis. His life's work re-inforced his belonging in a rare, celebratory way – as the best of his poetry did not. The fineness of the war-poems lies in the breadth of their humanity. And the direct transcription of exceptional 'ordinary' experience. I learnt of my father from them, who was stationed at Scapa with Keidrych: 'Duststorms sand up all skyline visionary.' Thus the condition of our human existence. I am glad to see these uniquely authentic poetic documents collected together at last.

Jim Perrin, St. Nazaire, Gwanwyn 2011

INTRODUCTION

I

William Ronald Rees Jones, known as Ronnie to his school friends, formalized the process of becoming Keidrych Rhys in a solicitor's office at 30 Quay Street, Carmarthen, on 26 June 1940, in the presence of Dylan Thomas. He and everyone else had been using the name Keidrych Rhys for some time, but it wasn't until 1940 that he changed his name by deed poll, so legitimizing a process of self-presentation and mythologization that had already become one of the preoccupations of his poetry. Taking his new first name from the geography of the region of his birth, Dyffryn Ceidrych, but opting to spell it with a non-Welsh language 'K', he had consciously reformed his persona, whilst reinforcing connections to his origins, and to the landscape and history of his native land. Whether the likelihood of an imminent call-up to the army had focused Rhys's mind on the need for legal recognition of his assumed name is at least a speculative possibility.[1] We can be specific about this small aspect of biography in the midst of war as there is a legal document to record it, held amongst other documentary fragments of a life in the National Library of Wales.

It is also common knowledge that Rhys was responsible, as founder and editor, for the pioneering Anglo-Welsh magazine *Wales*, which was published in three series from 1937-39, 1943-49, and again from 1958-60. *The Van Pool and Other Poems*, his one slim collection of poems, was published in the midst of war in 1942. He edited two war-time poetry anthologies, *Poems from the Forces* (1941) and *More Poems from the Forces* (1943), and in 1944 he produced the pioneering anthology *Modern Welsh Poetry*, published by Faber.

But much else that has been known about Rhys is more disputable, contentious, and elusive, including, until now, both his date and precise place of birth. Keidrych Rhys was born William Ronald Rees Jones on 26 December 1913 at Llwynyrynn, a farmstead of Bethlehem, Carmarthenshire, to Morgan James Jones, a farmer, and his wife Hannah Margretta Jones. Rhys's parents, along with his only sibling, Mary Elizabeth Eirlys Jones, who died aged only two of croup on 5 April 1919, are buried in the grounds of Bethlehem Chapel.[2]

Rhys attended the county school at Llandovery, where he received what he later regarded to be a very English education. Writing in 1948 he commented:

> When I tired of the Sixth form of my County School at the beginning of the 1930s [...], I had invited a certain amount of Anglo Saxon, lots of the French Romantics, hardly any Welsh history, although the author of the *Making of Modern Wales* was born and brought up in a farm in the neighbourhood and the only recognisably sympathetic reference to my native county in school and library literature had been accidentally found in the *Forsyte Saga*, that glowing account of a tramping holiday in the Van lakes [...] Evidently there was not much conscious or real national literary feeling in the Principality at the school level or even in the 20 page papers just then – the liberation of a long pent up Celtic-Cymrie feeling was yet to come.[3]

Looking through some of Rhys's notes and notebooks from the 1930s onwards it is possible to trace his determination as a young adult to rectify this Anglo-centric literary education; there are pages of lists and jottings on Welsh literary history, revealing an autodidact determined to master a tradition at once familiar and distant, rehearsing names from the early medieval onwards, grappling with the mechanics of Welsh language verse forms, and working out his own style of Anglo-Welsh *Englynion* and *Cynghanedd*.

As a young man Rhys had started out at some distance from his later literary life. Until 1935 he had a short-lived career as a banker, working for Barclays in Llangollen, and subsequently for the foreign branch of the bank in Liverpool. However, on 23 April 1936 *The Times* newspaper ran an article about a particularly odd event, reporting on a case at the Central Criminal Court in which Rhys, under his then name of William Ronald Rees Jones, pleaded guilty to a charge of being armed with an offensive weapon and robbery on the night of 26 March. According to the report he met and went back with a woman to her flat, where he demanded money at gunpoint, brandishing an air pistol. She screamed and he ran away, but he subsequently accompanied two other women back to their flat, where this time his threat obtained two shillings. The story continues:

> Subsequently Jones was met in the street by the first woman he had spoken to and he said to her, 'Don't be afraid; I have

got the money and I will not shoot you.' He got on an omnibus
and the woman followed him and gave him in charge.[4]

The report further explains that Rhys had left his banking job of his
own accord in April 1935, and in mitigation his defence lawyer
submitted that Rhys had undergone a nervous breakdown in October
of that same year. The following day *The Times* reported the verdict:
Rhys was bound over for the sum of £100 for three years, and
banned from leaving his home in Wales without the permission of his
father and the probation officer. Whilst this is an intrinsically curious
incident in its own right, it is also a characteristic example of how
Keidrych Rhys has so far been remembered and recollected in print.
The incident has become refracted through the vagaries of memory
and anecdote to become one of the often inaccurate 'biographical'
touchstones that portray a caricature of studied eccentricity.[5]

Much else of what Rhys did in his formative years remains in the
realm of speculation. Various potentially autobiographical jottings in
the Stanley Lewis papers and elsewhere suggest that he was present
at a Flight Training School for a while (not necessarily as a student),
and that he may have flown in Tiger Moth planes across
Leicestershire. Whether these flights are of merely imaginary fancy
or not, the experience of pre-war airplane flight recurs in a number
of his early poems.[6] 'Air Pageant', an early experiment in concrete
form, was published in the second number of Count Potocki de
Montalk's *The Right Review* in 1937, a number co-edited by Potocki
and Rhys's friend Nigel Heseltine:

AIR PAGEANT
Forty tuned planes
stretched crane-
wise across my sky:
arrows of plane-
shadows falling, lane
my cloudjoy's cry

Potocki was one of the more flamboyant figures with whom Rhys was
becoming acquainted in London. Born in New Zealand and claiming
Polish royal lineage, Potocki had been prosecuted and convicted on
obscenity charges in 1932 for attempting to have some translations
and verses of his own privately printed. He met Augustus John and
Dylan Thomas in the mid 1930s, and, funded in part by Aldous

Huxley, set up a small printing press in his flat on Lambs Conduit Street, on which he printed the *Review* in primitive fashion.[7] By getting into print in this and a variety of other magazines and reviews, Rhys was beginning to establish himself on the margins of the literary scene.

Rhys's earliest poem in this collection, 'Tenement', was published in *Comment* on 28 November 1936 by Victor Neuburg, the astonishingly eccentric poet, editor, and one-time friend of Aleister Crowley, who had earlier played a significant role in bringing Dylan Thomas to prominence and publication. The poem is characteristic in demonstrating both Rhys's predilection for poetic experimentalism, and also in highlighting some of the literary contexts in which he was trying to find a direction and a voice:

> and the street-corner meeting below
> and there that young red
> and living in sin
>
> clapse goes the cardpack
>
> and lip-lip decay-sharp
> and thins wainscot
> and damps of iron air
> and to howling kids
>
> (and the Have and Have Nots of means-test)
>
> frail on the threshold
> looking down
> on the concrete court
> and even on past concrete.

Neuburg added his editorial comment below the poem: 'Impressionism in tragic jazz; a new development. This poet, by letting metre and rime run loose, gets right in with his theme; unconsciously proving an absolute sincerity.'[8] Rhys wrote other poems in this impressionistic and disjunctive style whilst trying to find a more distinctive voice, and yet in 'Tenement' there is a real interest in the music of the words, and in amongst the modernist fireworks, a glimpse of a mind interested in the details of everyday life. The poem explores modes of ordinary and bohemian experience through the representation of a cityscape latent with poverty and sexuality, and of a potential, unspecified horizon beyond: 'looking down/ on the concrete court/ and even on past concrete'.

Whilst Neuburg was identifying something new in the poem, there is also at this historical distance a good deal of the anxiety of influence. There is indeed a social realism amongst the impressionism, but it is a poem socially engaged and obscure all at once. Rhys was influenced by, but never wholly subscribed to, some of the fast-moving, provisional, and overlapping movements, groups and 'isms' of this period, such as surrealism, the Apocalypse, and the New Romantics. Elsewhere there are traces of the very different but equally long shadows of Eliot and Auden cast over the beginnings of his poetic career.

However, the ways in which Rhys started to move away from modishness and confusion in the mid 1930s towards the discovery of a more distinctive voice had little to do with the influence of the metropolitan literary salon, despite the importance of this excitingly bohemian and down-at-heel world and his engagement with it. Distinctiveness, both as an editor and poet, developed from a determined and groundbreaking revisiting of his own Welsh culture and complex sense of nationality, and with the looming inevitability of World War II. What he took from his early exchanges with the London literati was a practical sense of how a small journal might be viable, important and influential. He gained further insight into how journals network, form alliances and cross publicize.[9] But Rhys's 'big idea' was geographically and politically removed from literary London, and is now widely accepted to have been an idea of significant originality and importance.

II

In his groundbreaking collection of essays *The Dragon Has Two Tongues* Glyn Jones wrote an open letter to Rhys, crediting him with starting the general enquiry into 'Anglo-Welsh'. Later in the book Jones reminisced about their earlier encounters:

> In 1934, as I describe elsewhere, I first met Dylan Thomas. In 1936 I received a letter from Crouch End, London, and signed Keidrych Rhys. That letter was the first of more than forty that were to arrive at our house from Keidrych in the next three years. Later in 1936 Keidrych, accompanied by a friend, himself turned up, tall, handsome, beautifully dressed in

country tweeds, as was his companion, and speaking disconcerting Welsh with the accent of the English public schools. This visit was the beginning of a friendship between us which lasted for many years. *Wales*, the first literary magazine of any standing, and standards, for Welshmen writing in English, had not then appeared, and Keidrych, its founder and editor, was looking around for suitable contributors. He had heard of me, he told me, through Dylan, whom he had met in London, and what he had seen of my work made him think I might be the sort of poet he intended to publish in *Wales*.[10]

Wales is accounted the first Anglo-Welsh periodical, and its influence and scope have ensured that Rhys's reputation as a journalist and editor has survived the test of time. The first edition, published in the summer of 1937, began with Dylan Thomas's apocalyptic prose piece 'Prologue to an Adventure', and included poems by Glyn Jones and Vernon Watkins. Rhys himself contributed two poems, and an editorial that set out a variously provocative agenda:

We publish this journal in English so that it may spread far beyond the frontiers of Wales, and because we realise the beauty of the English language better than the English themselves, who have so shamefully misused it. We are beyond the bigotry of unintelligent fascist nationalism. In case the English should claim our contribution for their own, we produce this pamphlet, calling it 'Wales' in defiance of parasitical adoption. Though we write in English, we are rooted in Wales.[11]

Wales thrived on this youthful polemic, and on the more specific political satire evidenced in Rhys's own contribution to its first number, his poem 'Cartoon Done in Something Will Be Done Week':

For Wales is far from beaten yet, my boy
While we all sign-on and save
Quaker Oats coupons for the grave.

At the point of choosing the back cover image for *Wales* no. 2 (August 1937), satire gave way to bald statement:

26% of Welshmen Unemployed
BREAD IS DEARER

England spends £1,500 millions on
WAR.

In another poem from the same year, focused on the state of the Welsh nation, Rhys registers the same concerns with industrial power and unemployment, but does so in a modernist idiom further concerned with the limitations of a certain kind of mythologizing towards a national identity:

> Ah Wales! your map is ribbed with living crossbones
>   (my inward revolt limned in tears)
> shunting crematorially despite the green incestuous laugh
> that blares and socks the oakgrown culture for Europe
> the by-pass message configurating the slag-heap moans
> the passive contour throttled by a fictional rendering.

>   ('Wales on the Map')

And yet for Rhys there seems to be an acute sense of the relationship between his own mythological 'rendering' on the one hand, and the immediate social and cultural realities of his situation, and the situation of Wales more generally, on the other. Certainly in the late 1930s and early 40s he was a poet in search of a connection between the mythic and his immediate context.

Rhys placed the poem 'The Prodigal Speaks' at the beginning of his collection *The Van Pool and Other Poems*, and in doing so he foregrounded an interest in origins and identities:

> Yes born on Boxing Day among childlike virgin hills
> Too isolated for foxhounds even explaining much more than
>   horoscope hours
> Far north of a fox-earth county never seen through rose-tinted
>   glasses
> Middle of war; hamlet called Bethlehem; one shop; chapel.

> Almost a second Christ! say; only son of a tenant-
> Farmer of hundred odd acres growing corn for red soldiers
> Merrily with a daft boy from an industrial school who
> Spoke in strange tongue across our great Silurian arc of sky.

The 'prodigal' is born into and out of a specific rural landscape which is on the one hand isolated, and on the other very much shaped by its political and economic contexts: this is wartime, and tenant farming is ultimately part of an Imperial effort. There is something vaguely Wordsworthian about the recollections of a rural childhood throughout the rest of the poem, reinforced by the presence of the simple consciousness of the 'daft boy' speaking in a 'strange tongue'. It also evokes a particularly natural grandeur: the setting of 'our great Silurian arc of sky' measuring the personal myth against the span of geological time, the Llandovery epoch of the Silurian period dating back over 400 million years. And yet it doesn't dwell on any one particular moment or image or narrative as a Wordsworthian recollection might; rather it registers in collage a whole range of related memories in quick succession, like a certain kind of filmic flash-image sequence:

> Deadly nightshade plovers eggs wind cool as air
> Under dairy slabs the tallest tree in whole Carmarthenshire

But this is a poem of remembrance where the past is another receding country that is viewed from and which contrasts to the prodigal's immediate present:

> Those secret see-saw spots that were our very own young
>   hearts
> Before deep crises and Eirlys dead puritans gipsies of yester-
>   day good-bye!

The poem ends by being valedictory, but that final 'good-bye' has to change the way we apprehend the mythologizing framework of the poem, however tentatively or imprecisely it is meant. For this is not the homecoming of the prodigal son, but rather his initial departure. This is not a myth of reconciliation, but of distance and exile from the past, and from a relationship to landscape, however the possibility of future reconciliation might be embodied in the shape of the Prodigal's borrowed story.

This sense of exile from a place of origin, allied to its central importance, is also a preoccupation of the poem 'Garn Goch', named after the iron-age hillside fort that overlooks Rhys's childhood home:

> Exiled by cruel tongues that madden blood
> I measure the now nostalgic needle hills
> Whose goodbye shadows now fulfil
> Their deep-charged love like Towy's flood.

I pack my things in a mountain gloom
Ideas of work in a broken mind
Of all a strange webbed future can find
In the pooled Van of a dark-eyed room.

In amongst the portentous darkness of a compromised past and an uncertain future there is the anchoring of the figurative life of the poem once more in an aspect of myth. The 'Van Pool' and its associated folklore is a subject that Rhys returns to in several poems, and which he prioritised in the naming of his poetry collection. The myth outlines a history in which the supernatural and the ordinarily rural come together:

> At the foot of the steep grassy cliffs of the Van Mountains in Carmarthenshire lies a lonely pool, called Llyn y Fan Fach [...] The son of a widow who lived at Blaensawdde, a little village about three-quarters of a mile from the pool, was one day tending his mother's cattle upon its shore when, to his astonishment, he beheld the Lady of the Lake sitting upon its unruffled surface, which she used as a mirror while she combed out her graceful ringlets. She imperceptibly glided nearer to him, but eluded his grasp and refused the bait of barley bread and cheese that he held out to her, saying as she dived and disappeared: 'Cras dy fara;/Nid hawdd fy nala!' '(Hard baked is thy bread: it is not easy to catch me.)'[12]

Twice more the widow's son returns to the lake, first with unbaked bread (no luck) and then with bread baked to just the right point (and the fairy lady agrees to be his wife). The lady of the lake's father emerges from the water and bestows a dowry of animal livestock, and sets the condition that if the young man strikes his new fairy lady wife three times she must return to the lake. Over a period of time the young man breaks the terms of the condition, and his wife goes back into the lake and all the animal stock return with her, but not before she has given birth to three children. These children, and their children after them, become the legendary physicians of Myddfai.

It is no surprise to see Rhys drawn to such a local myth: born in the region just below Llyn y Fan Fach, his childhood spent among the Van Mountains, he returns to his own experiences of farming mediated through this myth in his poems 'Letter to Lord Beaverbrook', 'Epitaph', 'The Van Pool',[13] and in 'Interlude':

The lady, the lake, both sleeping, the cattle
Called back through stories, bells silent, a deep down rattle,
Comics, rivers well-named, dense gorse floodlights the valley's
Gurgling. Grief in a mailbag; drama on trolleys.
Less and less shoeing for smith and farming's polite dying

In this layering of the mythic, the acutely observed natural world, the rhythms and motions of everyday life, along with a real sense of the immediate economic and political pressures on Welsh farming and rural life, his poetry shares common ground with the poems of his first wife Lynette Roberts, in which, according to Patrick McGuinness, 'Poetry is the mirror in which ordinary life looks to find itself reflected in myth.'[14]

III

At the same time Rhys was beginning to plan a career as editor of *Wales*, work he initially undertook from his parental address at Penybont Farm, Carmarthenshire, he was also furthering his London literary life, engaging with more magazine editors, poets, writers, artists and the bohemian group associated with Fitzrovia. His notebook records the following brief entry under the title 'Diary':

> 1936: intercourse with John, Empson, Thomas, Todd, Campbell, Duff, chiefly Calder-Marshall, Hamnet, Vinagradoff, Gascoyne, living in a basement, divan, extraordinary colln [sic] of books 'snowed up'; eccentric.[15]

In 1937 Rhys's portrait was painted by the Welsh artist Cedric Morris, and exhibited in March 1938 at an exhibition at the Guggenheim Jeune gallery in London, of portraits by Morris of notable figures in London life. Morris and Rhys were to remain good friends, although Rhys disliked this portrait and gave it to the artist Stanley Lewis as payment in kind to commission Lewis to portray him in what he perceived to be more representative light. Writing to Glyn Jones, Rhys announced: 'Cedric Morris has a show at the Guggenheim, including a portrait of *me*! Look like Auden. i.e. "queer"'.[16]

This notorious circle, with much of its life centred around the pubs and restaurants of London's Soho, was to provide company for Rhys at various points throughout the 1930s and 40s, and he turns

The Cedric Morris portrait of Rhys in 1937

up in cameo appearance in various memoirs and reminiscences of these periods: fellow bohemian and author Julian Maclaren-Ross describes drinking with Rhys and Dylan Thomas and making up drunken verse: 'Oh pisspot brimful to overflowing/ with milk of Keidrych-curdled kindness'; and Dan Davin has Rhys spoiling for a fight with him in a Fitzrovia pub: 'Keidrych's soft Welsh voice developed a note of menace. His leer was not civil, and contained no assent. I began to consider how, when the flashpoint came, I must upset the table against his thighs and get my blow in before he

Lynette Roberts's sketch of Keidrych Rhys

recovered his balance.'[17] Peter Conradi suggests Rhys got to know a young Iris Murdoch in wartime Fitzrovia, and that Rhys may have provided inspiration for Iris Murdoch's character Owen Secombe-Hughes, noting further that: 'John Bayley, who met him in 1953 or 1954, recalls Rhys as among the many war-time suitors who wished to marry [Iris Murdoch]'.[18]

However, by this time Rhys was already married to Lynette Roberts. Roberts was to recall being introduced to Rhys by

Tambimuttu, another Fitzrovian regular who published poems by both Rhys and Roberts in his *Poetry London* magazine, for which Rhys later worked briefly as London editor. Rhys mentions Roberts in letters to Glyn Jones dating from September 1938, and to start with it seems likely that theirs was a working, as much as a romantic, relationship. In one of these letters Rhys asked Glyn Jones to sub-edit a review that Roberts had submitted to *Wales* on the subject of Rhys Davies's *Jubilee Blues*, commenting to Jones on her 'untidy mind'.[19] However, in *Wales* no. 6/7 (March 1939) Rhys not only included Roberts's review, but also her poem entitled 'Poem Without Notes', which he followed directly with his own poem, itself addressed to Roberts: 'Ephemerae for Bruska'.

'Bruska' was Roberts's familiar name, also used for the flower business which she was running when she first met Rhys. She was engaged to man-about-town Merlin Minshall, who was divorcing his wife, and who it has been suggested was one of the models for Ian Fleming's James Bond. However, Roberts gave up the flower business, and Minshall, whom she described as resembling Tarzan, for a life of poetry and poverty in rural and soon-to-be-war-torn Wales, a decision that led to one of the great, and until recently, unsung creative partnerships in twentieth-century poetry. For an intense period of ten years both Rhys and Roberts found in each other and in their endurance of love and marriage in wartime a subject matter that enabled them to achieve a poetic maturity in distinctly individual, but mutually informed styles.

IV

Rhys and Roberts were married at Llansteffan Parish Church on 4 October 1939 only a few weeks after the outbreak of the Second World War. Dylan Thomas was Best Man, borrowing Vernon Watkins's brown suit for the occasion,[20] and Celia Buckmaster a bridesmaid.[21] Roberts, by all accounts, was always stylishly dressed. Argentine by birth yet of Welsh descent, a well-travelled, highly-educated metropolitan woman of the world, she clearly made a distinctive impression on the rural Welsh community in which the newly-weds decided they would settle. Even before the marriage proper she was attracting the kind of attention that Rhys was only half amused by, as he describes in a letter to Glyn Jones:

The wedding of Keidrych Rhys and Lynette Roberts at Llansteffan, 1939. Best Man, Dylan Thomas, is to Lynette's left.

Can't yet get over being engaged – it brings a smile to my face. Lynette says a policeman with a moustache at Llandilo told someone he'd like to meet her and has called at the hotel twice. Reminds me of the courting in one of your stories: I shall have to go and secure her.[22]

Their early life together in their rented cottage 'Tygwyn' in the village of Llanybri is well documented in Roberts's 'Carmarthen Diary' and in her 'Notes for An Autobiography', two accounts characterised by expansive and occasionally comic insight, which display the kind of annoyance towards her husband that only comes with true affection:

Today Keidrych frequently found cinders or grit in his stewed apples. I told him poets must always expect pieces of chimney in their dishes, that is their fate. He laughed and said what he usually does, 'You ought to be filmed.' His ears are scarlet and I hate him, he is always chewing humbugs.[23]

For a brief while they shared a relatively uncomplicated married life,

Life at Llanybri, with Lynette Roberts and their children
Angharad and Prydein (top) and tending the garden (bottom)

as reflected in Rhys's poem 'Section from the Van Pool (for my wife)':

> The Beautiful the wise
> plan for a simple life
> being married
>
> and as we strip-bath before
> the kitchen fire
> and cut moon-shaped and ingrown toenails with clippers
> wrapped well in Mrs Raymonds' towelling
>
> out of the edge of the dark
> one gets accustomed to a 4-months-lived-with body
>
> and your swollen breasts with the penny-plain markings
> are caught in the mirror of my eye

But this new life was inevitably and terribly disrupted by Rhys's call-up to the Army on 12 July 1940. He and Dylan Thomas had witnessed a conscientious objectors' tribunal in Carmarthen, but neither saw this as a potential way forward.[24] With the very significant exception of Roberts's miscarriage in March 1940 she and Rhys had been happily establishing a way of life, a writing career, a style and a subject matter. The immediate intrusion of war suddenly imposed a very different and inescapable subject upon them, which meant that both would have to deal, in their lives and writing, with separation, loneliness, the waste of war (both distantly and immediately apprehended), destruction, danger, illness, the questionable and imposing nature of Authority, and variously manifested suspicion and distrust. Rhys was to comment in his 'Introduction' to the first of his seminal war-time anthologies of poems by servicemen *Poems from the Forces*: 'It is a good sign, I think, to find our work very different now under raw altered values.' (p. xx.).

The War represented a new and crucial stage in their poetic careers, and several of Rhys's poems in *The Van Pool* deal with the early stages of his first-hand experience of combat. He became an anti-aircraft gunner in the London Welsh Regiment, and was variously posted to Scapa Flow in Orkney, to Great Yarmouth, and to Kent, not far from Dover, at a crucial stage of the war: he was there in 1940 in the latter stages of the Battle of Britain, and through the Blitz bombings on London and other British cities. Whilst there are some poems that focus exclusively on aspects of his combatant experience as a gunner, there are others which reflect on this experience only in the light of the effect that it was having on his personal relationship with Roberts. One contemporary reviewer, perhaps more unused than we are to the confessional and intimate possibilities of poetry, unkindly described these poems as 'exhibitionist', which takes no account of how moving and tender they are.[25] Consider, for instance, the recollections of 'Idyll on Active Service':

> Most I remember
> The grace of a womanly household
> Differences between home and bare barrackroom [...]
>
> Oh most I remember you
> Sweet mystery surrounded by light
> Worrying lost thoughts last words the dull birds might copy
> Suspense transition reconciliation that was so strange

This expression of homesickness and the insistence on the powers of remembering hints also at a falling out that had already happened. Roberts recalls in her 'Notes for an Autobiography':

> Letters fail to arrive from Keidrych. This was unusual as we have written to each other weekly. In the last he openly stated that he was taking a girl to the cinema and holding her hand. I was worried about the consequences, but admired his openness. I believed in being faithful to Keidrych and not kissing and taking hold of the hand of anyone else. He had moved to the anti-aircraft guns in Dover. There they had shelling from the French coast as well as overhead bombing. I would go and see him [...]
>   Something was wrong. Keidrych could not make love to me, he had got used to this other woman and their ways in the dark [...] I thought the best thing to do was to give him a tremendous kiss and I did this and he asked me to do it again.[26]

Rhys describes this reunion in 'Letter to my Wife':

> It was on the White Cliffs, my own, that we renewed contact
> Your image, flesh, bone, speech, thought, again became a fact
>
> Fine temper, home, and all unchanged yet stronger than
>   imagination

Unearthed, conjured – too much with the destructive tools
of reformation!

O marvellous personality – again we *found* each other
A living testimony of honeymoon outings together!

How I cursed the blitz in your hotelroom, affecting train and
memory

This passionate reunion is taking place in the immediate aftermath
of the Battle of Britain, and the continuing night-bombing raids on
London and other British cities. To be an anti-aircraft gunner in the
South East at this time was to be in a dangerous place; to visit a loved
one there from Wales, stopping in London overnight during the Blitz,
a widely-shared yet dangerous adventure. The danger is addressed at
the end of the poem, but the ending also looks to the importance of
striving at least to make things better:

Whatever happens, remember we strove for a more beautiful
world
When bombs come shrieking down *pray* men's minds might
be unfurled.

A similar championing of the importance of the personal in the
face of such public and ubiquitous destruction is seen in 'Alarm
Alarm', where a number of wartime combatant locations and
experiences are sequenced in a manner reminiscent of 'The Prodigal
Speaks':

All this I remember and more oh much more.
Digging planes King's Bench Walk The 'Temple' burning
But nothing nothing that I can compare
To love like a bell through Yarmouth flying!

Recollecting 1942, Roberts writes, 'I missed Keidrych dreadfully. I
joined him in Yarmouth and had to pass through London so I went
to Celia Buckmaster's home at Kings Bench Walk. I was astonished
to find the results of a raid were still pending after days.'[27] Rhys picks
up on Roberts's reported experience and elides it into his own in this
poem, but again there is the subjective subordination of these
momentous and destructive events to the importance of 'love', a
lyrical impulse most keenly felt in the context of war that finds its

echo in Roberts's poem about her own experience, 'Crossed and Uncrossed':

> Still water silences death: fills night with curious light,
> Brings green peace and birds to top of Plane tree
> Fills Magnolia with grail thoughts: while you of King's Bench
> Walk, cherish those you most love.[28]

V

On 1 November 1940 Roger Emile de Cannart d'Hamale, a young Belgian RAF fighter pilot was shot down during combat from 22,000 feet, crashing into isolated farmland near the Kent coast. Earlier that year he had been forced to bail out, and had survived, but this time one of the first Belgians to enlist in the RAF in the Second World War had become the last to be killed the day after the 'official' end of the Battle of Britain. Rhys's poem 'Death of a Hurricane Pilot', published in *More Poems from the Forces* in 1943, draws on his first-hand experience of arriving at the burning wreckage of this plane crash. It finds its analogue in Roberts's recollections of rushing to the scene of a crashed plane near Llanybri, an event recounted in both her Diary, and in her poem 'Lamentation': '*Dead* as trees quivering with shock/ At the hot death from the plane.'[29]

In Rhys's poem there is a quiet sympathy extended to the crash victim without sparing any of the horror and the pity of war, and also recognition of how both a private and a public life will continue regardless. He imagines that news of the airman's death will be assimilated, however painfully for some and glibly for others:

> Some woman will receive the fatal wire tomorrow
> A son or young husband cut off in his prime. Aged sorrow
> Will reign within the walls of a double heart
> And the experienced writer will reap his professional part
> With a prim or cultivated poise, the formal touch. In *The Times*.

Here is a detailed reportage, and in the absence of knowing the identity of the crashed pilot he anchors the poem to the particular geography, and to the details of army communications:

> And a map-reference will be given phonetically over the
> radio telephony set by a sergeant

Hurricane – Smersole Farm – Swingfield – field N.E. from
       farm buildings
Field behind stack.

But there is often a political purpose to elegy, and Rhys also reflects with grim satire on the way in which the description 'lions led by donkeys' was by no means relevant only to World War I:

A brasshat arrives.
                          Dreaming like a Brigadier
(At Sandhurst with Tiger Gort in '06)
Of cavalry charges with sabres, cold steel, Hore Belisha
And other terrible devices for polishing off the Huns.
But the winsome infantry of his imagination are as obsolete as
Were the fine Polish horse-guards
                          And he is old – a golfhouse drunk.

Inasmuch as this represents Rhys's later, more mature poetic style it is characteristic in offering a variety of observations and perspectives on its subject, clear-eyed in its detail and terribly aware of the brutal pity invoked by its subject. This poetry is being informed by the practised eye of good journalistic reporting and evaluation, and there is a voice here, and in other poems such as 'Air Raid on East Coast', that does justice to its most painful of subjects.

That clear-sightedness and journalistic currency provides Rhys here with a different kind of poetic register to stand alongside his engagements with myth and legend, and his committed investment in the poetry of the natural world. In all of this he arrives at a mature and distinctive voice, and at what one might have imagined to be the beginning of a more sustained poetic career. But whilst the experiences of army life gave Rhys a poetic subject, they also made writing itself problematic, a realisation that he voices in 'On Being Invalided Out of the Army'. Rhys found his way to Northfield Military Hospital in South Birmingham, which was being used during the war as a progressive army psychiatric hospital, and which had become a kind of 'Craiglockhart' for a Second World War generation of writers. Robert Hewison writes:

The artists and writers were themselves also eccentric; indeed, those of military age had to be in order to be there [Fitzrovia] at all. Rayner Heppenstall's novel *The Lesser Infortune* (1953) describes his meeting in Fitzrovia no less than three writers who had been discharged from the Army after passing through the Army's psychiatric hospital at Northfield, outside Birmingham, where he had himself spent some time. The characters, 'Dorian Scott-Chrichton [sic]' and 'a Welsh and a Canadian poet' are Maclaren-Ross, Keidrych Rhys and Paul Potts, who all became fixtures of the scene in the later part of the war.[30]

Heppenstall and Rhys had been friends and correspondents for some years prior to the war, and it is clear their friendship survived this most unlikely of reunions.[31] But discharge from the army did not signal the end of Rhys's war, nor of his writing about it. After 1943 he was employed in work for the Ministry of Information, and Rhys's movements across Europe in the later stages of the conflict are recorded in 'Bardic Crown Ballad', and in 'Victoria Leave Train':

mile on mile

A flush of correspondents sit like migrating swallows
Unaware of the mapped forest and the assembled shallows
Watching the beginning of one more trip to the End.

In 1943 Rhys was also able to publish *Wales* once more, which had been dormant since the winter of 1939-40. This second series ran through to October 1949, and consolidated Rhys's reputation as an editor of exceptional abilities. In 1944 Rhys's anthology *Modern Welsh Poetry* was published by Faber, although Rhys claimed they suppressed the long 'Introduction' that he had written for this formative anthology of Anglo-Welsh verse. Perhaps of even greater significance was Rhys's setting up of the Druid Press, based in Carmarthen, which was responsible for the publication of *Wales* through this period, but also for some important books, including Roberts's *An Introduction to Village Dialect* (1944), John Cowper Powys's *Obstinate Cymric* (1947) and R.S. Thomas's first collection of poems *The Stones of the Field* (1946). This creative period also saw the birth of Rhys and Roberts's two children: Angharad in May 1945 and Prydein in November 1946.

However, life in the years after the war proved far from unproblematically happy. Rhys's marriage to Roberts ended in 1949, when Roberts moved into a caravan in a graveyard at Laugharne with their two young children. During their initial separation Rhys stayed briefly with the artist Stanley Lewis and his family, where he was to

Angharad Rhys, aged two, with a proof copy of *Wales* magazine

abandon his notebooks and a good deal of correspondence. Rhys's life subsequently took him back to London, where he worked for charitable organisations, as Welsh correspondent for *The People* in the 1950s, as editor of *Wales* once again between 1958 and 1960, as a civil servant administering war pensions, and latterly as a bookseller, working from a basement room in Hampstead. He met his second wife Eva Smith, who had moved to London in the early 1950s to work in publishing, and they were married at Hampstead Registry Office in 1956. Their son Myrddin was born in 1961. Throughout these years and until the 1980s Rhys kept up a wide circle of friends and acquaintances, still acting as impresario and promoting the talents of Welsh creative writers and artists wherever possible. He and Eva remained happily married until his death in 1987.

VI

Although Rhys was most active as a poet in the years before, during, and just after the Second World War, two late poems included here see him emerging from what had become a comparative poetic silence. 'Aberfan: Under the Arc Lights' is a complex kind of elegy, written and published within a few days of the 1966 disaster, which characteristically combines contemporary experience with myth ('Ceridwen's cauldrons'), but also registers a further complex sense of belonging and distance:

> Ask what was normal in green nature and its pain:
> Will rain undermine our homes and us again?

Despite the deeply-felt inclusivity and affinity of these opening lines, the events are being revealed to the world and to the lyric poet in turn in one of the first significant live news television broadcasts. The technologies of a modern world refract experience through the partial lens of the television camera, and the effect is complex: part of it is to turn pain into spectacle, and to create a passive 'audience' against which the poem remains humanly active, with its repeated invocations to 'Ask', however painful the question, and however silent the response. 'Violence: Wales: 63-64', the other late poem included here and published, I believe, for the first time, describes, in ballad form, and with various satirical intent, the struggles against plans to create water supply reservoirs in Llangynderyn, Rhandirmwyn, and the Tryweryn valley. This in part takes Rhys back full circle to the valleys and streams of his native Carmarthenshire, but there is no nostalgia in the description of the immediate political subject:

> Next week year again will flame
> Violence; historical as reason,
> More terrible, notable, recent

In this, as so often earlier in his poetic career, Rhys is responding poetically to immediate contexts and current political affairs. That much of his poetry is elegiac in nature is perhaps an inevitability – a result of his seeing so much of violence and destruction on active service, and a result of feeling perhaps somehow often in a kind of exile from a point of origin, however intangibly expressed. However, at the same time his writing is innately conscious not just of lost things, but of how the past – historical and mythic – shapes a way of understanding a present and a potential future.

Since 1987 various obituary notices and subsequent articles have gone some way to evaluate Rhys and his work, but in this they were constrained by a distinct lack of coherent information and available material. Sam Adams writing in *Poetry Wales* repeats a story about how Rhys claimed that the typescript of his autobiography, funded by a Welsh Arts Council bursary in 1969, had been stolen 'along with his best shirts' (an anecdote, minus the shirts, and with a different bursary date, that opens Glyn Jones's very affectionate 'In Memoriam').[32] John Harris describes Rhys eluding him by giving him the slip in a series of planned meetings in which Rhys was supposed to unlock the secrets of his life and bibliography: 'He strolled past Hampstead underground station, a *boulevardier* in white shoes, precisely as I emerged from the depths. We exchanged a few words in a nearby lunchtime bar, agreeing to meet later that afternoon in Keidrych's new bookshop. He never arrived.'[33] Rhys himself had not been averse to adding degrees of confusion to his own picture. In a proof copy of his entry to *Who's Who in Europe*, dated 11 May 1964, he included the names of two additional publications to his usual list: *Angry Prayers* and *The Expatriates*.[34]

Whatever the accuracy of these various surviving accounts and vignettes Rhys was certainly not at all concerned about the conservation of a 'legacy', or about what posterity may or may not make of him, and the elusiveness of many of these descriptions finds its echo in Rhys's brief appearance in *Towers Open Fire*, an experimental film-short from 1963 by William S. Burroughs and Antony Balch. Towards the end of the film Rhys is sitting at a table with a row of men in suits, each one of whom is made to disappear before our eyes in a scene of apocalyptic erasure. He stares briefly at the camera before disappearing in a white shadow.

This collection is part of the reconfiguring of Keidrych Rhys: here for the first time his poems are brought together, poems that balance the lyrical with the enforced epic of history, that negotiate the mythical in relation to immediately apprehended experience, and that continue a distinct Anglo-Welsh poetic tradition, for Keidrych Rhys, soldier, editor, and poet, remained 'rooted' in Wales wherever else his paths took him:

> For pith, fruit, stones, for ghosts of a pickled hill
> The seeming everlasting light, vibratory, undulating
> Cut out of this valley, or felt
> For the illusion and the natural pleasure
> I wish you could have been here too, Eirlys,
> To have it painted on canvas for good
> You, only you, could have caught that riddle
> That blue afternoon's farness.
>
> ('The Van Pool: Tichrig')

Notes

1. Despite living at Tygwyn cottage with his wife Lynette Roberts, Rhys gave the solicitor his parents' address: 'Penybont Farm, Llangadog, Carmarthen'. In her Diary entry for that day Roberts makes no mention of Rhys's visit to the solicitor. Her focus was the recording of work and play in the fields surrounding the village: 'A child scratched a pig's back until it sat down in ecstasy, whilst another child set a trap to catch a goldfinch'. Later that day, thinking of the migration of birds, she was moved to consider her own situation: 'where shall I go and when? For instinct cannot altogether guide those who are caught in the chains of culture and a barbaric civilisation [...] we are at war so there remains only "chance" or fate to guide our footsteps.' *Diaries, Letters and Recollections*, ed. Patrick McGuinness (Manchester: Carcanet, 2008), pp. 24–25.

2. Meic Stephens's invaluable entry on Rhys in the *Oxford Dictionary of National Biography* is not to be found under 'Rhys', but under 'Jones' (with Rhys given as a pseudonym). The entry records Rhys's date of birth as 26 December 1915; place of birth Blaensawdde, near Llanddeusant. *The Times* obituary of 27 May 1987 also gives the incorrect 1915 as date of birth, but gives place of birth as 'Bethlehem, near Llandilo'. Almost every precedent and subsequent published source repeats a mistaken date and/or place of birth.

3. Keidrych Rhys, 'Welsh Writing 1938–1948', unpublished talk, National Library of Wales.

4. 'Women Held up with Air Pistol', *The Times*, 23 April 1936, p. 11.

5. 'Not to Leave Wales Without Consent', *The Times,* 24 April 1936, p. 6. Rhys's friend, the artist Stanley Lewis, was later to recall that Rhys had told him that he had once held up a prostitute at gunpoint, and that he had done so to achieve notoriety.

6. See, for example, 'Spin', 'Rip Van Winkle' and 'Cross Country'. Valentine Cunningham spells out the 'characteristic concatenations of '30s motifs and emblems – airmen, mountaineers, mountains, eagles, leaders, aerialism, and so on' in a chapter that briefly mentions Rhys and two of his 'flying' poems. See *British Writers of the Thirties* (Oxford: Clarendon Press, 1988), p. 155.

7. See Stephanie de Montalk, *Unquiet World: The Life of Count Geoffrey Potocki de Montalk* (Wellington: Victoria University Press, 2001), esp. pp. 211-16.

8. *Comment*, vol. 2, no. 49, 28 November 1936, p. 183.

9. For an account of how some of these networks operated see James Gifford, 'The Poets of *The Booster, Delta,* and *Seven*, 1937–40: Recuperating Literary Networks', *ANQ*, vol. 22, no. 3, Summer 2009, pp. 42–47.

10. Glyn Jones, *The Dragon has Two Tongues* (London: Dent, 1968), pp. 33-34.

11. *Wales*, no. 1, Summer 1937, back copy.

12. Edwin Sidney Hartland, *The Science of Fairy Tales* (London: Walter Scott, 1891), pp. 274-5.

13. The poem titled 'The Van Pool' is notably not included in *The Van Pool and Other Poems*.

14. Lynette Roberts, *Collected Poems*, ed. Patrick McGuinness (Manchester:

Carcanet, 2005), p. xxvii.

15. Keidrych Rhys unpublished notebook, Stanley Lewis papers, private collection.

16. Letter from Keidrych Rhys to Glyn Jones, 13 March 1938, National Library of Wales. The portrait by Cedric Morris, with its pupils poked through as a result of a mischievous child's modification, is still in the ownership of Stanley Lewis's family. My research establishes the artist and the provenance of the portrait beyond reasonable doubt, and the portrait's survival is revealed here in print for the first time. See *Cedric Morris: Portraits*, Catalogue of an Exhibition held at Guggenheim Jeune (London) [March 1938]. Rhys's portrait is listed as no. 39 of 50, and dated 1937.

17. Julian Maclaren-Ross, *Memoirs of the Forties* (London: Alan Ross, 1965), p. 148; Dan Davin, *Closing Times* (London: Oxford University Press, 1975), p. 4.

18. Peter Conradi, 'Iris Murdoch and Wales', *The Iris Murdoch Society News Letter*, no. 19, Autumn, 2006, pp. 2-8. Conradi further adds: 'Murdoch kept in her album, and so presumably valued, a photograph of [Rhys] wearing, if I remember rightly, tweeds.' (p. 5.)

19. Keidrych Rhys to Glyn Jones 12 January 1939, National Library of Wales.

20. See letters from Dylan Thomas to Vernon Watkins 29 September and 8 October 1939 in Dylan Thomas, *The Collected Letters*, ed. Paul Ferris (London: Dent, 2000), pp. 472-74. Thomas wrote with typical bravado: 'I don't suppose you'll be able to come to the wedding, which is a pity because we will make a party to go over to Ferryside and get silly. Send your rice anyway. Keidrych's parents are making difficulties, will not speak to the Bride, (she's very untactful & talked to K's mother, who's a hard-fisted old Welsh farming bitch, about colour-values. She doesn't know yet how to behave. Will Keidrych teach her, do you think? He's a very nice chap. He should tell [her], "One more colour-value from you & into the Ferry you go."), are talking of disowning their only son & won't attend the ceremony. I am to be best man. Have you got a respectable suit you can lend me, or, rather, trust me with?' (p. 472). Rhys's parents did attend the ceremony, and Thomas got to keep the donated suit. Letters from Rhys's mother to her son in the Stanley Lewis papers present an alternative view of a solicitous, doting, and generous parent, often facing difficult circumstances.

21. The novelist and artist Celia Buckmaster (1914-2005) worked alongside Roberts in her florist business in London, and made contributions to Rhys's *Wales*.

22. Keidrych Rhys to Glyn Jones, n.d. but between September and October 1939, National Library of Wales.

23. *Diaries, Letters and Recollections*, p. 3.

24. See Paul Ferris, *Dylan Thomas* (London: Hodder and Stoughton, 1977), p. 172.

25. Leslie Phillips, 'Poetry This Year', *Kingdom Come*, vol. 3, no. 11, Winter 1942, p. 42.

26. *Diaries, Letters and Recollections*, pp. 216-18.

27. *Diaries, Letters and Recollections*, p. 218.

28. *Collected Poems*, p. 21.

29. *Collected Poems*, p. 9.

30 Robert Hewison, *Under Siege: Literary Life in London 1939-45* (London: Methuen, 1988), p. 70.

31. In a letter to his wife of 28 May 1943, Alun Lewis reported: 'I had lettercards from [...] Lynette yesterday. K. has been discharged from the Army ("health reasons", she says), Maclaren Ross and Rayner Heppenstall are in the same mental home as "K" was. What's the matter with the boys? Can't they take the same knocks as everybody else? I feel a bit cross with them. Don't give K any new poems, Gwen. He's "funny".' Alun Lewis, *Letters to my Wife* (Bridgend: Seren, 1989), p. 357.

32. Sam Adams, 'Keidrych Rhys: Welsh Literary Impresario?', *Poetry Wales*, vol. 40, no. 4, 2005, pp. 27–32; Glyn Jones, 'Keidrych Rhys 1915–1987: In Memoriam', *Poetry Wales*, vol. 22, no. 4, 1987, pp. 12–15.

33. John Harris, 'Letters from the Cultural Battlefront: Keidrych Rhys and the Western Mail', *Planet*, no. 65, 1987, pp. 21–26 (26). For other accounts and reminiscences see John Harris, '"Not a Trysorfa Fach": Keidrych Rhys and the Launching of *Wales*', *New Welsh Review*, vol. 3, no. 11, 1991, pp. 28-33; Peter Elfed Lewis, 'Poetry in the Thirties: A View of the "First Flowering"', *The Anglo-Welsh Review*, no. 71, 1982, pp. 50-74; Peter Smith, '"Prologue to An Adventure": Fifty Years of Keidrych Rhys's *Wales*', *Poetry Wales*, vol. 24, no. 4, 1987, pp. 7-11; Alun Richards, 'Keidrych – A Memoir', *Planet*, no. 104, 1994, pp. 20–26.

34. *Angry Prayers* is indeed a book edited by Rhys, although it contains no significant writing of his own. It is a report on the Convention of British Animal Protection Societies from 1952, published in London by Canine Defence. Rhys, used to editorial rabble-rousing, contacted the literary great and the good, asked for their support for the 'cause', and subsequently printed their replies at the start of his report. T.S. Eliot, O.M. wrote: 'I thank you for your letter of the 22nd, on behalf of what appears to be an extremely laudable cause, and regret that pressure of other work prevents my contemplating attendance at your Convention in April.' Eliot's elegance was not matched by novelist Miss Ethel Mannin (the editor wryly tells us this is an exact transcript): 'I've no idea where I shall be next April – here in my Irish home, I home. I dislike cruelty in any shape or form – I even dislike cruelty to humans, wh most 'animal-lovers', I notice, don't – anyhow they support wars, & mass slaughter of their fellow humans. I also notice that most of these 'animal-lovers', so concerned abt pussies & doggies & trapped bunnies, have no objection to *eating* the said bunnies; not to mention piggies & the sweet little lambies & dear little calves...when they can get them. No, I'm afraid it's not up my street all this. And in an atomic age strikes me as an anachronism.' *The Expatriates* exists as an idea partially realised in notebooks now held in the Archive in the National Library of Wales, but the project was never completed – although the idea of a critical account of expatriate writers to include Samuel Beckett and James Joyce helps further to contextualize Rhys's poetry and its preoccupations.

A Note on the Text

This edition represents the first collection of Keidrych Rhys's poetry since the publication of his slim volume *The Van Pool and Other Poems* in 1942. This is the first time that Rhys's much larger body of poetic work has been collected together. Rhys's poems were scattered to the four winds of the twentieth century, and despite a number of partial bibliographies of Rhys's work much of the research for this book involved painstaking searches amongst obscure and transient poetry periodicals from the 1930s and 1940s. As such, this edition significantly extends the existing bibliographical knowledge of Rhys's work, and collects together poems that are unknown to a modern readership.

In addition to the sources of published poems there are three main archives of Keidrych Rhys's papers, which include several unpublished and incomplete poems, some of which are published here for the first time. These archives are held in the National Library of Wales, and the Houghton Library, Harvard University. The third, and extensive, archive of papers is in a private collection, and is referred to throughout this edition as the Stanley Lewis papers. The latter papers only came to light as a result of the research for this book, and they represent a significant resource to current and future Anglo-Welsh literary scholarship.

The explanatory notes indicate the known publishing history of texts where available.

Original punctuation has been followed, but obvious errors of spelling and typography have been silently corrected.

If any reader is aware of any further poetic material by Rhys I would be grateful if they would contact me at c.mundye@hull.ac.uk

Acknowledgments

My greatest debt of thanks goes to Eva Rhys and Angharad Rhys, who have provided inspiration and encouragement throughout. I am grateful to Jennifer and Bev Heywood for their generosity, friendship, and recollection, and for access to the Stanley Lewis papers.

I am grateful for the support I received from the staff of the University of Aberdeen Library, Bodleian Library, British Library, Cardiff University Library, University of Delaware Library, Houghton Library, Harvard University, and the National Library of Wales. The Keith Donaldson Library, University of Hull provided me with invaluable assistance throughout.

The photograph of Keidrych Rhys's wedding is reproduced by permission of the National Library of Wales; Lynette Roberts's sketch of Rhys is reproduced by permission of the Harry Ransom Center at the University of Texas at Austin; the portrait of Rhys by Cedric Morris is reproduced by permission of the Estate of Cedric Morris. The portrait of Rhys by Stanley Lewis is reproduced by kind permission of Jennifer Heywood, and the photographs on pages 27 and 34 are reproduced by kind permission of the copyright holders, Angharad and Prydein Rhys. The poems 'Tercet and a Lyric Interlude' and 'Hanes gwaed ifanc y tywydd' are published with the permission of Houghton Library, Harvard University.

Many other people provided invaluable advice and assistance in matters of fact, interpretation, and translation, including Huw Jackson of the London Welsh Centre, Patrick McGuinness, Angharad Price, Jacqui Oguzcan, Meic Stephens, and Sue Stone. As ever, thanks to Anna Fitzer for her support, encouragement, and insight.

The Van Pool and Other Poems
(1942)

THE PRODIGAL SPEAKS

Yes born on Boxing Day among childlike virgin hills
Too isolated for foxhounds even explaining much more than horo-
      scope hours
Far north of a fox-earth county never seen through rose-tinted
      glasses
Middle of war; hamlet called Bethlehem; one shop; chapel.

Almost a second Christ! say; only son of a tenant-
Farmer of hundred odd acres growing corn for red soldiers
Merrily with a daft boy from an industrial school who
Spoke in strange tongue across our great Silurian arc of sky.

Cloudroll over flying brontesque heights; this early photo
Fiery enough this rusty pocket-knife recall now
A two-mile walk to school alone along a Roman road
Geese-fright on common the little sempstress staying a fortnight.

Wheels scotched below the varnished meadowlands
A jack-in-the-box handed down from a badly-
Loaded trap back from market town steaming pony
Gentle to touch mad dual-purpose bull in lane near thing

Lost to parents for days every summer on black mountain
With endless views once faint after first experience moral
Deadly nightshade plovers eggs wind cool as air
Under dairy slabs the tallest tree in whole Carmarthenshire

Where hedging match meant more than holiday by sea
Stitches at sports then poaching salmon Ben Christmas
Dan Joshua the bastards how hold gun snipe otter – bobs
Are symbols to a returning self like mushrooms-in-dew oh balm!

Country folk all goggle-eyed outside a wedding inn
Damp dusks scarecrows whirring in a flickering light
Those secret see-saw spots that were our very own young hearts
Before deep crises and Eirlys dead puritans gipsies of yesterday
      good-bye!

POEM ON BEING

Looking out of the storehouse window
At the gradient through the firs
At the house built of river stones
At the tiled hill on my ordnance map.

Hearing the noise of three plain pullets
Upon a rainwashed cart
Someone emptying a bucket near the tap
A wasp glued on the pane, that barrier.

Gripping a boyish pen, the buzz in my head.
Inside harness hanging over milk-churns
Our first pony at the station driveway:
Feeling good and cheerful with nothing *much* to say.

THE GOOD SHEPHERD

(translated from his own Welsh)

Go and spy on the sheep
My father would say
Before I went to school every morning

Today snow covers the ground
On field the sun shone
And the fat sheep cut the trodden patches

I counted them
I looked at their tails!
I found one new lamb and put him to suck

In the zig-zag shelter
Of the hedge by the crooked cart-road.

I smoked a cigarette
That the hired man gave me
There was a lovely slide across the river

I scared the sheep
I bulged after
Through the gap to Old David's cow pasture

Teacher said I never polish my shoes.

INTERLUDE

Simply I would sing for the time being
Of the wayward hills I must make my feeling
The rickety bicycle, the language of birds
Caught fishing up the church street for preaching words,

The deacon hawking swedes, the gyppos clapping on
Their way to vans over common's crushed sandstone
And the milk stands so handy to sit upon!
The roadmen laying pipes of local cement
The Italian's chip shop and the village comment
'No reserve; all they know on the tip of their tongue.'
That educated tramp from the lodging-house league.

The lady, the lake, both sleeping, the cattle
Called back through stories, bells silent, a deep down rattle,
Comics, rivers well-named, dense gorse floodlights the valley's
Gurgling. Grief in a mailbag; drama on trolleys.
Less and less shoeing for smith and farming's polite dying
'Messiah' in the chapel – but a warning, gulls crying
Up at Easter miners off the race's soothing colour.
Oh simply simply I sing down the masterly contour.

THE EMIGRANTS

Disguised in Sunday suits they left
Like flakes of snow scraped off your breast
In February. Rollers from Guest Keen's
Fitters and surplus families
And sons of rough-haired Vale of Towy
Farms, with golden Pittsburg maps, with
Patagonian holdings in their dreams.
Relatives tell of the sad farewells,
The pathetic send-offs at this station.
('Crowds like those at rugger-match trains.')
Mencken, too, notes their influence
On his language, their two periodicals
At Utica, their surnames in Manhattan's
Phone Book, how they clung to native
Speech.

The Valley News in spent bullion
Reports how the Wales colony
Fearing the danger of the rising
Generation capitulating to the
Spanish way, and their breaking
Their religious ties with the homeland,
Once invited the honoured Rev.–
(Nice dithering bardic minister)
To go out there, to preach Welsh Gospel,
How his name is revered in that
Far corner of the globe, his mission
Standing out in histories of
Nonconformity. How on return
He lectured at Literary Societies,
His innocent impressions full of
Original reflections on men
And life and having a fine literary
Flavour.

How these mysterious religion sexes
Claim legendary neutrals, swarm
Do their expectant letters home,
Charged with Brython stipends,
Whose orgy of music drove
Madog to an Indian land
Many Boer-centuries before Ericson.
Tomorrow napoleons pack
For Dagenham and a Trading Estate.
Do you not shed a tear, Dai mon!

BARDDONIAETH

(For J., D. and D.)

Dee is back from the English hospital
with servant girl ghosts in maternity ward
where they still believe in that highland regiment
which returns in a storm to their ever-long words

Dee brings baby; babies change like a breeze or
jaywalker's tree and mothers should not really change
babies like David who from now on will not change for me
and perhaps mother as well in a world of strife and Jaw;

out on a lawn of songs in the family pram
staunch at his bottle of milk; a gipsy; warm-weighed;
– over breakfast – 'he began crying at five' – o you little dru–
surely you will break many an Allenbury's chart

far off on air torn by thunder before he stops
final visitors, presents, 'fixed' by his right open eye
and frowning lines; seven on temple; two on chin;
his hair! – his chest! – 'you love babies?'; no, no rocking, that is sin.

David, magnificent name, sucks like Musso; kilted; deep in his rosy
          shawl,
deep in cot's oblivion, screened from river, fight and toil.

POEM FOR A NEIGHBOUR

In the sea-marsh where I carve the harsh shallows
On the turfed rock rise a shock of willows
Stockdoves, fireflies, sea-gulls, bats from the hollows.

In the sea-marsh where outlaws starve with my Molly
On open knoll scrolls of black alder sea-holly
Instead of the screech-owl's extravagant folly.

In the sea-marsh where the buzz-hawks' talk is drover,
On sea-pulses, rag tag, lurking circles, clover,
Love-sick flicks light the nightmares of our half-drunk lover.

In the sea-marsh now springtime graves new paved with dew
On Ovid's buckler a trysting moon to Tresaith grew
Winnowed the heathcocks, magpies, cranes, sea eagles flew.

LETTER TO LORD BEAVERBROOK

At five o'clock
in a harvest hurry,
I drive the herd out of May aftermath,
busy with stick about the drinking trough in the rough flood-yard
where the big blue-grey fresian behaves like some playful bull
near crazy when exercised each Krooshial morning:
– here the dog snaps gentlier at heels
as slowly into an enlarged cowshed intent on its three
        walled-up doors
they move, in cowlike fashion
like a wonder, say, from a mythical lake under Towy's source:
now all are chained and staring up unknowingly vacant
resembling a knot of 'grinning peasants off the Black Mountain'
oh how this next phenomena saddens me!
this sudden straining of wild eyes as I measure out
their oil-cake-ration
... grass supplement for summer feeding mineralized
frightening the third bloodstained kitten eating rabbit remains
in the enormous bowels of the calves' loose box
– killed by a chalky mother
a long white watch over a far hole
two days, three days, ago.

My obligations are as timeless as a vet's
(I can't ever make out the Land Army hereabouts somehow)
a flannel rag for washing teats the warm bucket of water
and then to see if the water tank is pumped full
a traditional procedure in a walk of life
that's got such a lot of prestige! unfortunately it may hold
little recompense nothing but toil for the old for the young

still when you're young it's another story ...
it's no good stroking the best beast's forehead.

Yes, I hope I am your solitary agent in the country parishes
but in the erect cemented sunlight what can one do
except take waterspout weight off too-long-weighted shoulders
unless unless...

For
who cares a damn about farmers anyway
anybody outside the *Daily Express*?
We could be as happy as honeymoon couples? With a little money
to spend, with a little leisure, in an unlean, uncalloused hour.

Perhaps even the bright halloo of Simon Lee again
but who cares a damn about farmers anyway
nobody nobody ... only the *Daily Express*.

WEEK-END IN SOUTH GOWER

Tin plate rust slips by. Streamers of smoke, pale blue,
Puffed out, flee our course making slow muscular turns
In sky's sham light. Soon, down, by level and deep shades
Powerful sea birds arch over; out, a gale bellies;

Thrives on sleep, for the house is perched on a cliff,
A summer suntrap steep to a pencilled bay and
Faraway fawn sand chop: a jackdaw is clenched
In a nerve window – not real any more but no fake.

After breakfast, a trawler stops opposite, while we,
My host in foreign shorts explore broad-in-chest caves,
Pwlldu, the hidden river: this winter's ring on stone
Wooing the echo beside wet and wood, and soil more loose.

Now the stiff climb, some duck-necked oyster-catchers.
Recall a poet's haemorrhage at base; talk bosh.
Watch specks move up towards sight-seers' crags, so we, late
Just before teatime dare go, and I, a wind-in-jawbone man

Like madmen, busy, pass over our mutual heathgrass,
Mark rock on trees, small ponies at their toilet,
The housetops round Pennard Castle, that single sentinel.
Appetites for evening palate when croquet is played.

How easy drown all rivetting here and one's own fluid iron side;
Fowls, wired, flat; the rusty rivers of descendant worlds –
Over buttered toast! A miserable enough bus ride back.
Yet my happy ghost-in-hell would haunt no coast. A sad thing.

SPIN

Pupil pilots groping in bourgeois bars this red night
Reversing the signposts' gaze and letting off rockets from
    the policeman's garden.
Riding in forbidden cars, sluicing down in the depraved
    bathroom after sprinting over
Wet aerodrome grassblades to bungalow in canvas shoes
And this in forty flying schools not built on fertile swan's
Or holy ground where formations cut up myths like air.

I am sad:
       I am he killed
On his first cross-country solo:
                         a mass of tangled
Iron on a sky-pulled field. The local papers give me, a picked boy, a
    column
But at the same time ask for others (with, maybe, a bonus after
    four years).
At the enquiry it appears something knocked out – and yet
There was the ambulance ticking over at the
Hangar's side.
       Death, nerveless, collects one's wreath from
    friends, prepares our nerves for war.

SECTION FROM THE VAN POOL

(For My Wife)

Half awake I lie in tearful Llanybri
Hearing the midnight birds' full-throated cry
in the hand-attempted trees
opposite;
unimpeded I attempt, thinking
of places well-visited by the imperial sun

Geraldis: regionalism:
the Sleeping Bard; proselyting:
makers of history all

under cirrus sky the tower turns
round onto Brazil, spurns
the Spitfire swifts down underground
becomes our early-morning sound
where the wrung heart is a lost marriage hurt
oh her skin smelt sweet, smelt sweet
and the family in the Plata estancia now;

birds fall
in showers
write on the wall
'it's war, it's war'
all is glitter, bitter glitter

O if I could penetrate your ear
penetrate the regions of spontaneous fire
and enter
read thoughts, walk about your brain
to forget the world's derision
O the image the image is surely written there

the peasant's gift
the dog lapping up water from a tall bucket
Gardening: tiffs and anger
gospel ideologies
faith and the stirrup county

two people striving together
helping each other
and living happily
in a bridal chamber
I thee worship with my body
war-wedders
self indulgent vicar
we eat & drink the trousseau's inside us
and the furniture list money no fuss
but now the ironic bells no longer invite us to church
fondling a fine blueveined hand
the photo: the fights
and a beautiful wife in bed

You don't get any pleasure out
of the hyacinths in the flower pot
says she
        head rolling on divan
in elementary rhythm
dashing off an airmail,
when will we Latins sail?
draw up hammock and deck chair?
what we do do do is
go out and watch planes banking
over the castle through binoculars
                     &
happy unquestioning
Farmboy lovers in Spring
Happy minds! in tight-kneed village tailored trousers
Ogling,
Sizing
Up the Post Office girls from the Square!

cousinly congratulations outside Llandilo market
schoolboys catching trains as I did once
the music-teacher taking the bus to a remote pupil
totem and taboo: the wedding ring

Llanstephan – sunlight on the rambling roof
    in early morning
    different rooms
    bedlinen – cool sheets
  the visit to the woman on the Langain road
       soldiers in Carmarthen

  Proo Proo Proo
    a farmer calling
  cows – against the blackbirds' morning screech
  some have a feeling for inanimate things
  and see the sensuous horse-block eating grass

pleasures are known emotions on parade
the regional way of life
uppermost in Vale of Towy!
   the remover's van furniture
   thank-you letters posted off on a Sunday
   2 Chalk dogs

The Beautiful the wise
plan for a simple life
being married

and as we strip-bath before
the kitchen fire
and cut moon-shaped and ingrown toenails with clippers
wrapped well in Mrs Raymonds' towelling

out of the edge of the dark
one gets accustomed to a 4-months-lived-with body

and your swollen breasts with the penny-plain markings
are caught in the mirror of my eye
frustration can't create
oh what material for a none such novelette

I wash slowly from the tepid pail
Everybody in Llanybri washes on Saturday night
Marriage is not a Hollywood comic
as Mrs Rowlands the widowed daily help knows

back up the fire for the night with 'pele'
see the china crockery alternate on the dresser signifying snows

and then to see my joy clutching the cottage banisters
upstairs to a patchwork bed

we test our dangerous ceiling from the table
    And now
the world is as deaf to us as print.

GARN GOCH

Exiled by cruel tongues that madden blood
I measure the now nostalgic needle hills
Whose goodbye shadows now fulfil
Their deep-charged love like Towy's flood.

I pack my things in a mountain gloom
Ideas of work in a broken mind
Of all a strange webbed future can find
In the pooled Van of a dark-eyed room.

LETTER TO MY WIFE

I eagerly await your miniature, wish the artist would hurry
For morning and evening I want to look at the girl I did marry

I will wear the old-fashioned locket (cum-identity disc) always!
Although this must seem a little sentimental for nowadays

But after all I'll simply have to hang on to my identity
Otherwise how carry the sayings and small things for posterity

It was on the White Cliffs, my own, that we renewed contact
Your image, flesh, bone, speech, thought, again became a fact

Fine temper, home, and all unchanged yet stronger than imagi-
        nation
Unearthed, conjured – too much with the destructive tools of
        reformation!

O marvellous personality – again we *found* each other
A living testimony of honeymoon outings together!
How I cursed the blitz in your hotelroom, affecting train and
        memory
O white breath on air, your teeth are still naked pearls assuredly

Life before meeting you was a drifting chaos, pretty purposeless
Needing your sturdy Argentine warmth to fire me on, loveless!

After film-dawn halos, a too short union, now we've been
        9 months parted
By circles of lust, still threatened but O how amazingly lion-hearted

I miss your letters terribly when our mails go wrong
Those days are blank for me, the sky without a song

You are my front-line love – and always will be – with *ease*
Oh I can see you at your window in the cottage through the trees.

O ecstasies of courting days O clouded quarrel-days
The Fuehrer wants a word with you! the simple life the simple Joy
        just stays

(Vision somewhat tamed maybe by the spirit of youth
Still I only want you, and peace and a home in the South.)

O My Darling and my own
       Remember the willows by the river in summer
       Remember always our love in wintry weather
       Remember the cottage the bridge the flowers the fields
       O never forget the power love yields and wields

Whatever happens, remember we strove for a more beautiful world
When bombs come shrieking down *pray* men's minds might be
       unfurled.

POEM FOR A GREEN ENVELOPE

I blunder between huts in the 'towards' dusk
on the way to the coalheap to fetch boilerhouse coke
and ponder pawls and cams and differentials
and our record breaking boxline monkey barrage
identification of planes Deanna Durbin's popularity discussed
not much to make for a personal philosophy
that wishes most for time and tranquillity
But I have faith in these men greater than in artists as friends
ah of those twisted beings I can't say 'I like the present breed.'

For in the morning the bowl of gunfire is handed round so gently

But too soon I stumble over rough ground to the guns
slip past the Command Post dragon flag to the tune of whistles
respirator under arm, shell in fuse-setter for tray
inside emplacement report
'Ready for action'
under the extraordinary blue of the breech-light
warm hands at the white of cartridge-shell cases
while others place cooled charge-cases aside
and box them methodically
oh surely we won't go back to a pre-war world

every night killing becomes more automatic
as we rest huddled in beach huts like animals
writhing in the equality of barrackroom language
taking the piss out of OCTU Garnett the covent-
garden whitening-haired porter
who's now on the danger list on a hospital-
ship poor man with a large family
and the celebrities the soccer professional the zylo-
phone player, Tich with cauliflower ears,
Danny Williams, the rhythm brothers, Jack Hulbert's
collaborators – the ex-war policeman
Chaplain to this misshapen staring mass

Lord, awaken me from earth, stitches in side
Lord, snap the bloody chain around me.
Or are you another piss-and-wind orator?
Why do we fight?
Oh make it stop.
Stop IT!
Brigade confirmed three totally destroyed last night
the Hon. Colonel Sir Henry ap Rhys Pryce says
we have a good name at the War Office
But isn't the new barrage too deadly for chivalry
although it is good to be alive
how the bullets flew – two notched the Lewis Gun-
handle – and look at the tents sandbags emplacements
Is life a bowl of cherries or
'a dynamic equilibrium maintained through an
unitary semi-isolated system?'
Do not expect too many new images
I'm doing my job as it is!
My it's good to find the sun, the sea, the once-
gay seaside house & suburban extravaganza
as good as to love nakedly like a tree in the afternoon.

      But
Grim as death says some
grimmer say others
brothers who cut no comparative ice
joyboys compressing the springs of action
those 'I-don't-happen-to-be-one' restraining
Or those who when younger
Risked death obscurity & hunger
And all its attendant miseries
To cut that marauder's rope
Rather than be bruised lives in Injustice's hope.

People expect a revised death attitude & impersonality
expect one to greet spirit-friends of a far-off future
a reversed seance
kept out of themselves, in sunshine
but it's examination of equipment, turning handles,

drills for adjusting seat, an elaborate Xmas dinner menu,
full of Skinner's rare humour,
Old Testament misquoted etc.
But this war is also certain, big, & strange &
here I am unbefriended in a bare land.
O is it from these:
 the Red in the ranks spouting
 destructively – revenge for past wrongs
 the boy with a turn for inventing
 the north country lad swearing by Cornish vagaries
 the girl windlassing in slacks
 sweet betrayal of the last suffragette
 Springs the Future, the Future.
and so it goes on
beautiful salvo lovely salvo
magnificent resplendent splendid bursts in the moon
tin hats sit delighted on brains

oh we poets write & write & write until
we write what we don't feel
crusading. It was thus when
we spoke & said what we didn't mean
crudely in the fast wire till nowhere elate
the patterns of our lives converge like Fate.

Now waves of greyness descend on the camp penetrate the Nissen
 huts.
Let me go out in the dark
 dark dark dark
& be alone in its chill seagirt unknowable ground
& escape the surfeit of barrackroom friendship & laughter
 with its attendant petty irritations
For then the soul can find itself comes back in
 on its own destiny
For then sudden ghosts like casualties seem reassuring
 in these dark camouflaged environs
Where lurks no perplexed wanderer
 no swimming weaponless enemy
 lit up by horizon's horizontal searchlight clusters
 nor mines unfriendly

Oh my loved ones liked the dark and sea

The dark most tiresome in its vapoury patches is
                              wholly explicable

Now intensity is all
To us confined in camp construction
With a detailed knife hanging over our heads
Ghost of ego-wishes
Delightful concretion of peacetime vision!

THIRD AND FOURTH

When stone-hewn storms knock against our cottage,
What shall we do, my love, my love.
Prove the aspirations of the fourth generation?

Soft buckets from the ivied coalhouse
Out of a too-dear two hundred weights ration
Sitting dusty in seven-day cindery contemplation.

Sprawl on peasant divans on the gingham-checked cushions darling

It's war. How shall I feed my unborn baby
Now I'm unemployed and have no money?
Breast feed him? – we're a civilized country.

Lord be good raise a fire in both rooms
Light up the books and rugs the pots and pans
But what if the rain-drops seep in at windowsill
And the wallpaper is damp and dripping?

Is it our nine-days Wind-baby howling outside the house-walls?
Now when the garden is old-audacious with snows
Must we put up black-outs against heaven's carpentry?
Prove the aspirations of the fourth generation?

What shall we do, what shall we do?

The retired tavern-keeper is seated alongside our primitive
        villagers under idiot oak-beams
Dismisses the tainted ravings of our poacher-hating farmer
With the double-barrelled B.S.A. shotgun
But should poets half-use binoculars?

Shall I phone for the country G.P., have first-aid ready?
The hot water boiling, a towel. Everything sanitary.
Say: I fear a miscarriage: not diet, worry.

Out of the window, a stack, the cowshed, the smithy.
Ssh! Are you quite happy?
You miss me when I go out of the room.

Announcers and Messerschmitts exhale over our Welsh earthsmells
Can't bale out in an Irving: Haw-Haw poisoning the wells.

Dusk's hushed figures slink in the doorways of darkness
They're carrying jugs of water, they're breathless
The pink limed cottages cluster mysterious
Around the four-cornered tower's stillness.

Cast down by hollow suffering I recall
Children in the shade of the Old Chapel wall
The schoolmaster buying a packet of fags at 'the Shop'
Kisses on nape of neck pass for a test of heart
in a time of cynicism and rum
So many, so many are longing for husbands to come
up and squeeze them to their hearts

But here your dear warm afternoon body remains
Proud against pillowslips cross-colour pains
Three wardrobe gargoyles stare at where
Two golden-winged cupids look down from above
        in their rare profusion of hair

Look down upon what cut our bed of love
My love my love what is to be done

O darling shall we curse the Hand above
The Hound of Heaven, the bitchy Joy master,
And the cheap carved bum-dimpled Bacchus, be tried
By all the fertile nightmares of felicity which cried and lied:
Be interrupted in the flame of midnight by demands –
Imagination hearkening along bumpy catcall lands
... And once for months, Oh absent months with tears
Quick tears, I sickened for your off-blue whiteness!
No. Step out of shoulder-straps marriage resurrects holiness ?
Who saddens us now with bellowing... ties also the clover-gift?

Does the storm abate its puffed-cheek breath, then start again?
Who says:
There is a spot moving somewhere in air?

Is there no-one no-one no-one to prove, prove aspiration
Prove the aspirations of the fourth generation?

I ponder too long the X-ray child in his mother's womb.

IDYLL ON ACTIVE SERVICE

Most I remember
The grace of a womanly household
Differences between home and bare barrackroom!
Discovered little possessions as an aid to happiness!
How busy were my peering trying eyes!
Where leaves and stones and waves are hidden
But the trees were green and stood up naturally
There's (I found) no formula to deal with life's problems
Especially for fools frightened of making a bloomer

Calm and collected on a frontline vulnerable point
Playing at Cowboys and Indians
To please Generals
Where dusk's bombs trick flesh and eye and the windy
While you expect unruffled prose as frank expression
When we younger people are as powerless as static words.
Has war taken all joy out of life?
you might well ask
And left just a blankness and an accepted bitterness?

Oh most I remember you
Sweet mystery surrounded by light
Worrying lost thoughts last words the dull birds might copy
Suspense transition reconciliation that was so strange
how beautiful it all was then
even for one so tired and sleepy
the sense of landmarks set in roadways
the exhilarating comments by the way
her hair her hair her hair

and the village cat now mine
sits squarely on my shoulder-blade
invasion bone of myth
purring like a highly emotional time-bomb.

SOLDIERS IN SCAPA

I watch the plovers wheel low at dusk
Over the sparse-sown grass
Where soldiers trample with lobster-pot cricket bat
Into the wet canteen for a last drink.

Out of the blue of this 'sunny' island
Landlocked our padre walks, and chats
Of the native pleasures enjoyed in this land.

The islanders somewhat narrow, farmers,
Less interesting than the sailormen Shetlanders
How they eke out an existence God alone knows

Duststorms sand up all skyline visionary

Guillemots fishing-flighting across the narrows
Suffer more from boredom than silenced I;
Bird-winged – a floating island of despair, sure – the bay
A dark mind conditioned under Northern Lights.

O will millions know troopships destroyer escorts again
Ploughing past the roughed greenlands like explorer's boats?

Except in the great white motion of natural elementary flight
These tireless sea-geese rockwards go, so far
Defenceless – like a Harrovian brigadier's map-mind.

Orkney, May 1941

LAMENT

(In Memoriam T.J.M.C., killed flying October 10th, 1941)

Worse than branched antlers in the blood stream
Worse than the tapping pain of madness in the veins
For grieving mother is her boy's death
In the smoke-plumed spinning reaches of smooth air

How soothe her inconsolable soaring cry
When we are dumb of tongue and see too clear
How know the often-dull 'touched' scatter-brained fraternity
Now other than as semi-godlike heroes
    near-sons dear-ones yes no less?

Worse than the licking dearth the limits of her great emotion
A range out-topping earthly Reason is this small
    jubilant death and this great grief.

SWINGFIELD NEAR HAWKINGE

In these simple headstones in this green churchyard
I discern a rooted way of living, salt of earth
Parallel to ordnance lines in the parish of my birth
Good husbandry bequeaths vows no bully can retard
In this burgeoning autumn; now a man's reputation for
Open-handedness, is no stern a reminder in this waste of war.
When incendiaries serve only as souvenirs in village inn
Of ruin spelled to a farmer and passionate fighting
For one's own spot, inheritance and all, doomed by a cocktail
  breadbasket
Spread over a fruitful county, that nature in her wisdom met
Well-being gutted, barn-places burn-out, literal sucking pigs
White-oak waggon in open cart-house no more than cindered twigs
Three fire brigades brought own water, crossing 'field' shoots
With the ground slippery mushy giving under our gum-boots
A sporting man, he worked for slow returns, gave awkward
  hospitality
But over the trip-wires at the edge of the wood his lonely sheep
  remark on this latest inhumanity
And the oldest inhabitant centred in the village hall dance
Knows the brave (some local lads) who fell in France were never
  cruel
Therefore they have the Porch in the lovely old church as memorial
  Instead of a prim rectangular grave
  Or a shallow sandy Libyan grave.
Noon: lightheartedly looks the light on the parkland trees
And in assured sunshine a traitor's remains lie charried in the
  breeze.

GENERAL MARTEL

Shortish, active, gay, dapper in a British Warm
Hiding too many personal griefs perhaps –
With an extraordinary charming smile
For statesman, equal, or for the merest trooper
Beside his modern Hussar horse under trees' shade.
Calling at the War House in a ranker's battledress
On a curious project of no strategical account
– My sole encounter with the high-ups!
I met you straight from a Lord Mayor's wartime lunch
And a parade through the City – minus introduction,
Not that your open sincere understanding needed one.
Your mission – to modestly ask the Press cut out
The reference to you as one of the greatest
Generals in the world! I remember that much.
Then someone mentioned another 'good general
We lost in Libya' – one of the best – you agreed.
Yes you certainly possessed that Tank Corps 'madness'
Properly fitting for the Royal Armoured Corps' Commander
That you largely built up. There I saw you embodied its
'Identity' and 'soul' radiating a mystique that will yet
Blast the enemies prepared cannon-fodder
And that will make you beloved among slant-bereted heroes and all
        men.
An engineer who saw in Force a power for Good
Which the safe-living civilian could never realize
While others were talking glibly of King and Country if of anything
Who when first-time equipped could smash through the hot-
        housed Panzers
And with a frank face that belies a valiant soulful spirit
Human and gentle, exuberant, 'a brain.'
Surely a tank was your first love!
Whose biggest fight was against the dead hand in the black years.

Sometime after I saw your face on a magazine cover.
THE MAN AGAINST HITLER'S TANKS. I believed!

FRAGMENT

Writing is difficult in today's shrill air –
A dear kind of puppetry – under juniper shade –
Beyond our real selves; heart utterance is loss,
Revolts others – a pretty, though improbable, keepsake:
The naked heart (alone) eyeing with natural grief
Is swift, covered by erratic snowflakes, the tented
Folds of flesh slacken onto hollow belly
Sheet shivered against blanket on bed:
                              This is the Nought
The final upward adventure, our great enemy,
Imagination wreaks revenge on all dilettantes; hate
Is next lover's torture on underside of penny myths
The violent outcrop-prerogative of Abelard's eternity.
Above tumult – no sleep-release; your womanly shape
Escapes like ghost; a cornered image tucked to left; mind
Like fortunate in Convent; child's play in field; as in Burne-
Jones's hoyden heyday: Letters speak to me of spice lands
Where you remain too long between wind and sun – find music on
Morrow, while here farm buildings harbour a small country's soul,
And I alas! am left behind half dead with my Welsh sorrow.

COMPASSIONATE LEAVE: FOR BRUSKA

Count ten hours hollow on soldier disc;
Replace tear bottle in its drawer;
And watch our bronze-cheeked Cupids mask
Satan off, while I sleep beside her.

TRAGIC GUILT

No. I'm not an Englishman with a partisan religion.
My roots lie in another region,
Though ranged alongside yours.

But I can sense your stubbornness and your cohesion
And can even feel pride in your recent decisions
That anger reassures.

I know no love for disembodied principles, improbable tales.
The strength of the common man was always the strength of Wales,
Unashamed of her race.

May this be also England's role to bring to birth.
May she draw opposite new powers from the earth.
Huge Shakespeare has his place.

I have felt in my bones comradeship and pity,
I have seen wonders in an open door blitz city.

Amid tremendous history, new pity.

Uncollected Poems

TENEMENT

Bugs
symbol the
spirit
of the place more

spider-pawed
beetle-clawed
Fabre under the floor

patch the window!

absentee dust
toothed-secret

and the street-corner meeting below
and there that young red
and living in sin

clapse goes the cardpack

and lip-lip decay-sharp
and thins wainscot
and damps of iron air
and to howling kids

(and the Have and Have Nots of means-test)

frail on the threshold
looking down
on the concrete court
and even on past concrete.

WAR-BABY

daft daft is the alloy.
old men call me war-baby
their daughters   their darlings.
    'beauty is death my boy.'

    cast up the graphs booby.
siegfried and wilfred were big.
    cost ap rhys telegraphs trilby.
dylan and us want a rug.

    cover the bags.
    empty the dust.
were fed up with the skirts of booze-crazed love.
        tailor the rags.
        polish the rust.
please give a nod a kiss from a misspent grave.

    and of course X
    has heard of sailors
        who darned their sex
        round those lacy sectors.

AIR PAGEANT

Forty tuned planes
stretched crane-
wise across my sky:
arrows of plane-
shadows falling, lane
my cloudjoy's cry

BUILDING JOB

That public works stock galvanized priestholes.
Explanatory of bridges dams and docks
That reservoir an animation out of dykes
And royalties that bare our astral tolls

Now filed the bulletins once shot in daily strike
Shaking the outer panoramic mind veneer
The fake report, the cops, the cat velour
Are the comic reward to the student stroke

Reason the charge hands chucked the job in
Demand the shilling rise and ambulance lug
Five field stations employers interest blacklegs
All shown middays, and solidarities win

Remain 9 a.m. meeting outside the cemetery gates
Frequent breath born in tool conditioned filth
Brickies like others whirl through voracious wealth
Follow deputation with mute springline guts.

While the taxi weeds them on accident hire
There hospitals, first toadstools then as hoots.
Dinner. Two inches in water the wearing out boots
Of sprinkler chaps fooled with 1d. an hour

Beyond the hated dirty work, prophetic days
Of unanimous decision shed lustre. All futures.
Investment force with rotten boroughs gone. Natures
Built with these skilled hands, these sympathetic dyes.

RIP VAN WINKLE

Yesterday by surprise the unironed landscape
From the squirrel-trees (like acrobats
The raindrops) tumbled to Rapunzel
Over smudgy snow and garden dung
Comfort was gone from our valley

To-day the aeroplane breaks a furrow to Ireland
From the easy corrugated horizons
The prescribed sheds and council houses
Whose false teeth manage fingers of cake
Scattered valley still rich and still so derelict

WALES ON THE MAP

(To Bryan Elliff)

For crisake shut up you and your druid delights
blotting the arthuriana finals of one's cup
the viking silences over three-splintered seas
the troubadour's wayside joys on season ticket nights
as historic Norman voice meets Keltic chronicler's lip.

Send pussmoth crashing my unearthed thoughts of bards
the hammer of our fake professor adds not to folk-lore
the exhaust of the eisteddfod nonconformist
is robot flesh to injections, gipsy rennet that curds
the special area the commissioner's art missed sore.

Send home my sackcloth miners shipwrecked in the Strand
where political odds are not the joke they're at home
or where faces at the windows duplicate
faces early-old bending over moleskin without end
the freed grit from each lever sud of Time.

The heraldic past is the catalogue ting-a-ling
the syphilis graph often comes as a bethlehem gift
crinkling the factory bones reading racing papers
and still the shrouded voice of nostalgic themes sings
on to diminishing gorsedd returns but no night-shift.

The privileged missionary efforts of engaging buccaneers
the autograph hunting of negroes bearing grocer names
the sunken empire markets for Rhondda anthracite
the stacked-up chiming almanacks of Sir Alfred Mond
point to the jazz pattern, a class-clash after straw rugger games.

Still *sospanfach* always beats the national anthem
still the red demo is scientifically policed
Spanish conscious of the thunder of law and authority
regulating with the banker's idea of art and rhythm
the prizecard choir, a brass band after disaster mortuary laced.

In and out of the dance hall go the Valley girls – a film
followed by bible-class thighs in pressed dungarees
laundering the sixpenny entrance in the half-cut lights
that promise cramped love in squalid adventurings
a lorry-hop heaven like a Jubilee excursion to London.

At twilight to-night the No. 2 pit are holding a Lodge vote
the owners too have got together to counter-protest
the trout are restocking the polluted river
the silicosis-sensitive have barb-wired the anti-vivisectionist tote
and their new advertisement shines with an affiliation crest.

Ah Wales! your map is ribbed with living crossbones
        (my inward revolt limned in tears)
shunting crematorially despite the green incestuous laugh
that blares and socks the oakgrown culture for Europe
the by-pass message configurating the slag-heap moans
the passive contour throttled by a fictional rendering.

CARTOON DONE IN SOMETHING WILL BE DONE WEEK

Don't say we don't love Moseley and Houston D.B.E.
Kindly refrain or I'll get a slop to run you in – hey-he
for these can only be loaded at the Savage Club
pour encourager l'art, the Litvinov sub.

They radio Mr. Baldwin has gone to the waters
to discover a brand-new baby-poet, Marx Webber,
with a spa-pipe and a bowler-hat
the seven wonders now start

See them Intourist off
cough up your sleeve
at the sleeve of the toff
we can't relieve

'I heard yesterday' that ... alone
was kissing a long goodbye in the mirror
give the old cocker a bone
and save us the third terror

Double-barrelled he shot stuffed pheasants
to find what the whores charged more for
and the Finest Job joins Black Watch or
Slides our world to think of the first no ... of peasants.

Slogan: our coal is not so dusty: advance
forget his murderous paper-drives
catch-cries of hoodlum painopia droves
Go for the tom-tom winds its whip-dance.

II

King calls in his expert
perhaps to insulate the dole club
or maybe just to draw up another dud report

and here Novello
complete with cello
dials merry hellos

Content them then with supper-clubs and cottage hospitals
a lido and sixpenny chukkas
Bossed over by nice retired persons pukka

gentlemen what we need is black-and-white
in tins to tune our empire night-starvation
sir, we hereby ratify this cartoon of the nation

For Wales is far from beaten yet, my boy
While we all sign-on and save
Quaker Oats coupons for the grave

Come back a spring
said the foreman of the oilworks
Not a bloody cuckoo cried Dai's song

Dockhands prefer Three Nuns
of active curates on the arctic back
Who knows the bishops of Menevia wear West of England slacks?

And the nonconformist
of the kitchen drama
really you know my dear would scrum the Y.M.C.A. piano

Thank you so much
for speaking; do please come
again: I'd love another crutch

SOCIALITES

Here are the majors, putting up the bunting,
Too soon for wagers, too late for hunting:
How chiefs can run a nation's paper,
When moleskins MOH a draper!

THE FIRE SERMON OR BUREAUCRACY BURNED

Penrhos Aerodrome, Llŷn, Caernarvonshire,
Night of September 7th, 1936

This is a poet's story cut by the strong
Magic of a dominant land. Now, the real
Healers branded as quacks, the shut prophecy,
Forgotten like the unemployed, grows lungs
For scores of bards, for haunting elegy.
Simple faiths praying – England's gift a bombing school.

Llŷn was focus and native pinpoint. Doom.
Prize for patriotic verse. A super bandstand
For the coronation marching songs.
The half-goose built on, despised our heirloom;
Our paper jazzed up some toughs – refused our wrongs.
I want the world to know and understand

All, how the Fire was forced on the Three like royalty.
Taliesin, Their language they shall keep.
Literature was withheld in this nutty dam.
They burnt the Aerodrome and wrote why.
We wanted a hero with a drastic programme,
So they transferred the Trial to the Old Bailey,
So they could clap him in jail for so few days.
Time. At Llŷn a scarecrow smokes a gassy pipe.

CROSS COUNTRY

In aerodromes blue blades of grass
Leap into a warning shape
Good, contact, lunch, and gin in mess,
Speed lost, three-point landings made.

In coloured plates of aero mags
The war-crock fears a foreign speed;
They were crack; now romance lags,
No test ace doubts Italian leads.

Close-ups of sky engage trainees.
Prep school boys know all the carded makes
Two quid an hour dual amies
Get off in a club tea dance break

In workshops, logs, jigs, no fags.
Camera gun records are late.
At eleven the watchman begs
Woodbines, notes L.A.C.'s pass, shuts gate.

SPECIAL AREA

Now a heavy hand lies on my land.
Each finger a claw
Of anaemic blood oozed in the dunes of sand
That holds the paw.

And wristy hairs are sparse in a light
Drawn in the earth,
Knuckled with slagheap warts and pylons' flight
Shamed of their birth.

Where bodies masquerade in a thumb joint
To weather blots,
A cry of a puncturing fire pinpoint
Burns unused lots.

Tuned to a harp the tips are white in sun
Nerved to the seas,
They long for the cannibal life of guns
In a blood breeze.

SPILLING THE BEANS

(Dialect)

Spilling the beans you are bad voice; hard Diawl
Stoops in the paper wormwood from prompt Taffy
Like the slippy tinges of rag-trade pens.
Look you inteet, now that's for stricken overture
The divine go-getter in the cockle street
Sincere to Shakespeare's funny totter
True as a giggle that drums his mists of genius
To sip the bushy ointment of election beer
In some back snug: to Kiddies pear-drops
Weird as Lord Melchett, as jet roads of graft
And there that royal doctor's bed-pan farm
And this our hamlet where Jeremy Taylor cried
Yet bitter is minister's righteous mutter.
Hear you not gypsy the local poll results.

YOUTH

I try to remember the things
At home that mean Wales but typical
Isn't translated across
The Channel: I try to create,
Doors grow into masts, love losses
In the village wood, but boyhood's
Fear fled into the pale skeleton
Of the dark mountain, into
The bilingual valley filled
Through a sail-hole of my drying
Feelings. But I try. Lightning
Is different in Wales.

CYNGHANEDD CYMRY

Lips curry-flame
Byces henna foetor

Whizzing wizardings
a languor lingers
a slight slough
an even avon
hoary hairy
with the greengrins of a gubbon goblin
fig
X in an axe
split-peas and platespies
    among the river rovers
                or
      the shame of shimsham
      the shame in SHEMSHONG

By coarse beards of curse-bards
by the pore-hanger for pure hunger
by the heelhorrorhirry of hale hurry
by the fool-foal feel in the faaall
      a picture pasture for posture
      a NILE of nails
          simple samples of live love
          shun the shine
          flickers fleckers
              liftever the leftovers
              the far-tight under the fear-taught

Launch lunch in a glad shoeshy glade
with a pinch of punch
with our jane on june air
with the coif   the carafe   the neon-noon
    from

linden London

LANDMARK

Only the cemetery is landmark, all our pilots limbless
Fondle control columns cold and wax; night; half glide;
Rudder our ship to the deck in the T signal light.
Rumble in over the gleam of infant bones.

Be speed in my dream dark, drug winter schooling
Of drag menstrual years: draped in their sheets
I see the decoyed boys but stained: the darlings of their year
No longer lisp attractive, magnet no liberty.

From poles molecular, the artist's friend, who played the pub piano,
Detects boyhood's cherry red: inverted the furrowed vein from
      norms,
Colour, negro and Death's. Youth dreams. 'Don't leave me nurse
– (Sappho) seduced and lone. O where is the petalled hair and
      happy head?'

But priestlike each futility; pain cold no virgin's labour;
Brains all sucked and sacked, the hangers deaf,
Though there's the tragic dance of the coarse naked hangmen
In this cemetery of landmark, where the hairgods feed.

DURING LAMBING SEASON

Side by side let elder sheep roll over on spring earth
huts are dry and full in Talley, china blue eyes write signs of birth.
Here's work for boys in long corduroys from Mothvey to Golden-
     grove
all through that summer's rogue Ryland ram's brief nonconformist
     love!
Oh the young devils are tough with bleeding navels lean on ground;
by elements torn, brown hairstuff licked, prayer suck, born worth a
     £.
Wander off like postman, sex by chapel ballot to save funeral
     expense
Still no need to ridicule Sabbath morning pack out of existence.
Up on a ditch one inhales fag's smoke on account of hand closed
     flesh,
their ears are made of a god's carpet, cut out; a penknife mesh;
too weak you say, well kitchen fire, whisky in a silver spoon, ma's
     ah!
false baba sentiment! these parents wear no bells; but the same
     happens baa baa;
low-bellied, hedge-breakers, man's bloody marvel, organized on
     purple hill:
do it with an arm in a sling; drown to a rook's rainy stare; die of
     woolball.

THE LAST SUPPER

In the cavernous dark to see the chains
Pile armfuls of hay to divided mangers
Then out of two half-doors walk to the rear
And pull back hot dung to drain with shovel
Avoiding sudden kicks their swishing tails
When scattering bedding from a calf pen
Then swinging my stable lamp in lighted arcs
Fasten the hen house door with a meat-hook
Turn wick, to book and fire, dreaming *Bless the foxes*.

TRI ENGLYN

I

Sometimes it strikes me oddly how our farmers
might ungodly Breton fisherfolk be! dictators
descry a no-religion state! see armament kings
heap up gold plate with hardearned silver!

II

Minister of Agriculture gives his party's policy;
the opposition gull rural voters in the *Stockbreeder*;
even Bolshevia would bolster with watchdog gusto of Papacy;
like river tides seem the switch moods of each chosen leader
as I gaze at the imagined greencrop over my feather!

III

Old Llewelyn's hoax deluded the Law;
but when corn was ripe and hay fit
he cuddled the sportive girls in the straw.
Now in forty weeks law will take in wit.

FRAGMENTS FROM THE POEM
OF ASKING

In moleskin bags, string tied round their knees,
Faces newly washed
Blue-mottled like a bruise
They dribble their sing-song way
Along the sombre lane from bus to colliery

Immobile is the shift
Filled with fear of director
And death fall of roof
The crowded cage goes down the shaft.
Underground
No sprightly hewers of coal
Numbed in their stark tunnel
And dimly forgetful
Of their early-married wives
Their sores, a vague dozen
In the ragged toss of dark,
The shreds, the lamp, the tram,
They lean
Their emaciated souls, now frozen

HERE'S YOUR SOUP
BUT PLEASE DON'T BE CLASS CONSCIOUS

Insensible to boy labour
The woven venom of the chapels
Let only the over-worked mothers
Dulled at washtub
Scoop in bad housing
Why bother
With high infant mortality

EVERY COLLIER BOY IS SACKED BEFORE HE'S
TWENTY-ONE

Is it better as it stands?
Soldiers!
They sent you back from the trenches
For some skilled digging wages.
You are
As drugged slaves.

Horses, with less resignation,
Happy away from the buried stables
Fight to a sun blinding light
From their darkened gloom.

BEFORE HE'S TWENTY-ONE, BEFORE HE'S
TWENTY-ONE.

Once I read, in a novel of one of you
Who wished he could live
Like a mole
Away from the top
Away from care
In some black twisting gallery
He didn't expect
Sweating of parliaments
His weak hope lay
In the marching spirit of the pit

SOSPAN FACH YN BERWI AR Y TAN
SOSPAN FAWR YN BERWI AR Y LLAWR
A'R GATH WEDI SCRAMIO JOHNNI BACH

TRYST

Slender-slid lashings a-patterning the skiey waters;
Splash churned with under-thuds; blown clanging junketings.
See nowhen Spring uncovers, two lovers drop to bedearth;
Lie warmly; drip secret; woken winter dreams in twos.
Darkness slow pads her glow for eye glue, yielding shielding.
Spray spew, bib-throb bobbing-so; in shapely shower
Our flowering endgirl cowers flick-flushed, sea-mouthed to bone-
Painted like a suck-street index sister; plague spread
Ocean slopes sow talking hopes, bee-tongued; here make believe;
Grieve in ropes' sob-silence twig-naped; coned from prostrate
Fate, love-tocks; sunstrong in weasel frame when roofing rubs.
      Shun
Stun clouded stains; broken wave-noughts, devil spiffs to night's
      spoofing clubs
Shadow passionwork of all token, the nunhidden minutes.

BLACK TRUST

Rhondda belches across mind,
Stone play, out of smoke, set,
Fibre of industrial mess.

Moratorium raises signal hand,
– Coal, product, ships, met.
Leaves canker of hate in mass.
Tynesider   Clydesider
Cagewheel, crane on slipway,
Mind is torn, as others
                    Soot settles
                    in distance.

UNDERSTOOD BY BOADICEA AND KING ARTHUR

(to D.S. Savage)

In here-exiled with our private myth
With a tongue's survival against spoken word
The squalor-world, the fanned away

Cry turn others (illicit) around skull coloured
Sheer in corridors like a prince on probation.
– O what a shadow hangs rough over our headpiece?

In here-alone-some balanced guilt of home-ties cat-
Licks the long lost from Blue Masque Club especially
When fatal blondes leave Garbo's range; scared stiff.

If-next-oh the things one would ever do with money.
Discover sleepy worlds; a proper 'shift'; a new emotion
Mere man be almost horror-fine across

                         invisible blood
                          invisible fire.

NONCONFORMITY

The 'study' lamp burns through the minister's
glass; while soil has hardened his sermon tasters'
temper; travel is never suffered after
a soft wife – romance shunned like the young's tears.

The deacon's plate gold made during war
is simply eyewash: here is no pure mountain man
but someone less than human to ostracized sons;
the servant who soldiered bleeds kicked by this master.

TREASURY

Here are the goods. The footnotes the themes
Birds Spring a wave breaking on reams
Of waves. Flowers autumn nature in general
Play and war fairies and whatnots in overalls.

The village blacksmith is one up
On Herrick's daffodil sigh
Wordsworth next close-up
Hats off the flag is passing by

Remember bits of Hiawatha
That's the way for Billy and me
In the land of Willa Cather
Pippa passes Paul Revere's tea.

When shepherds watched their flock
The brook the fountain Old Ironsides
Pied Piper teases Inchcape Rock
And Bluebird charges light brigades

Under the greenwood tree
Somebody's mother views
Through a Norse lullaby
How they brought the Good News.

The wreck of the Hesperus
A child's thought of God
Or Abou ben Adhem's fuss
Lochinvar bugles odd

The Builders of the Voice of Spring
March and Jack Frost,
The fringed gentian bring
Mountain and squirrel lost

The Wind and the Moon
The French Camp Incident
Must be a boon
Now my anthology's spent

We're fed up: please teacher give us a ballad
A limerick fresh as green salad
Teacher we're tired: say a bloody nursery rhyme
Broadsheet folksong shanty and carols of crime.

LANDSCAPE PIECE

The car sped south along a coastal road:
Lleyn, to a long blue bay the calm desire.
Our learnéd sons have crossed the fearful border,
And now old men at home govern without fire.
Cardigan. O who can revel in that joyous peak
– Deep-sown the speech and hillbound the people?
Chapel on hill; prime ships of tombstone; all, all doomed
Like brilliant boys in metropolitan exile.
Northward snow waves were a shock to system
After smoking chimneys and welfare parks,
Derided by falling streets down to a shore
Where even furnace shapes blaze through trains at clerks.
Horsemen gone; earth bare: no sun shines bright today
On man of straw, foolish student, or his apostasy.
T.b. reports; a cometobed; or G.P. bomb.
No wonder our birthday stars have stolen away!

HOMAGE TO A SPLIT MAN

There are almost a thousand legends about him,
Some twisted out of all shape, preserved by toper, very odd
And handed down as gospel by the playboys of that period
Who somehow missed his mental strife and evident dual shim-
      sham.

Perhaps even the early facts are strange enough though true.
Blank birth in one of the four hotels; loathing both Eton and, still
      more,
Oxford: loving Cologne and music like a child upon sea shore
That just simply would rather throw up modern ships of war than
      animals for the Zoo.

To several novelists he looked wholly hideous; rain washed him
      clean.
He pub-crawled on the damages! His railing against chemical beer
Often upset police courts next morning as much as the Cafe Royal
      leer
And in-dense-air swig; against inward edge, a mere saint; then a
      singer without a bean.

Accordingly his legend grew and grew: his women rhyming and
      drinking.
His curious friends in the Paris studio; his fierce swilling in the
      country,
Unless you say it was his Elizabethan self, outside this dreary blas-
      phemy,
Worshipping exquisite blue-black devils and perverse with heroin
      and morphine.

Of sly song; but generous as a duke; a fiend in the ninth circle.
No, he never smoked; yet barred to burrs; always a man for sitting
      among
Dark evasions; tie askew; oh so changed! Jenny Lind is pinned
On those greeting walls; here a quick one; here a rhyme; still long-
      ing for the throng.

And the high dance; and the songs, published; and the paper he ran
Are all part of ghost searching half-starved through an artist's
ploughshare
And now his drunkard rows in Chelsea over don enemies do reveal
quite a split man,
Double remove from toughs with knuckle-dusters in a four ale bar.

Without a model in flux, he stuffed his shade; distorted, misunder-
stood, but news,
Actually suffered few d.t.'s; preferred red cats to barmaids swift
with lunches – was
Sought after, praised perfection in many ways; only late on found
every child pretty gross.
Guess. What was it? money? or sense of failure? did he turn on the
gas?

EPHEMERAE FOR BRUSKA

Stories of many slants, gods of sea and sky
Courted by whispers spotted in the wind
Where deepset eyes, still heroes, caught still older legend:
Many, as you know, long haunt lounge through guest house wind.

These, without apparent purpose; what the postcards say
Of their pictured leap over stone
She who taught a bird the word (a fly in my eye)
Or of Arthur's hound hunting boar and sow
Is rum. Though now dawn spirits squint at water's dawn stone.

Elsewhere the others were led astray on the mountain
According to plan; the scribble was only mountain –
A formula for a curse; and over the dwarf's grave
Stood the brindled mastiff, the dog guarding the cave.

Mound, well, hearth, then crossed; nodded the physicians,
Noted the lidded couple beside the misty lake
On their way to Woolworths; here a custom crossed; passed
The child-eating hag with a sprig of hazel; oh great yes great!

Except for mistaking the rowan in the cwm for apple tree
The marches stirred for our three breasted lover, also hill.
True this resembled other world witchcraft or banknotes; still
The florid were cured by yarn; the needy set free to marts.
And we learnt madness by degree and ate our fathers' hearts.

SHEEP

Limp in lambing weather
Sheep curve over shining snow
As collies command
And worry on the slow

Huddled in larch hurdles
Branded by index ear
Play for dog-trials
Again they wait in fear

Rinsed in mountain torrent
Held to shearing machine
Next disinfectant
Poking through of bone

Bane of braking motorist
Bound for peasant cottage
They winter twenty miles away
Beyond a Cardigan village

Behind – Cheviots of early start
Bleating of loaded truck
Sharp bids at Lampeter mart
And the smile of a butcher's cheque

CORACLE

Disturbed at night by marooned moos of flooded islands
We had a coracle man up to the model dairy farm,
(Llew carried *it* rudely folded on his back);

Now we paddle as pebbles in a closing valley;
In dirty weather Towy's staid peasant waters slide
And like Echo's shoed hooves shoo squire's Dandy;

As if stepped out of Antiquary's case-book
This latter-day Briton knew his slime-green rocks,
(Llew netted small trade at the river's mouth);

Here I felt the direct idea to a happier Wales,
The original argument against a machine century,
Broadcast by a licensed waterman of Carmarthen;

I lit the farm hands busy trucking Co-op cake
Free in a singing cave off Talley lake,

Queer sea-beasts startled the early-simian eyes
Of Tenby as coward's beer or a puritan curse.

SPELL

Chaos finds grandfather kinder than parents
Our blood in tune with a springing sap,
Despite glacial signs, the odd fish, not born in the heart.

Pure words seldom carry to the county border,
Beyond chapel walls a stile and a very black salute.
Frost. Shoni's easter-egg, the exile's Noson Lawen.

And boxers out of the pit allow the counting of drunks,
And the converted try of a beloved back.
Good to the slumming girl, the Sêt Fawr bureaucracy

Always. The squire in them is not wind in flower gardens
Which must be tired of such superior corgis
As we are of making a living in this dry-rot land.

Hand-in-glove rebel youths rub along crude of creed.
See! half a million strenuous kisses! hoist a tattered red dragon!

DEATH-DANCE
OR
CASE HISTORY OF THE LUSTROUS NAVEL

And so buccaneers *die*; placid; still; with certain grace.
(Death-love is everything to Sparkenbroke).
Even now pack lipsticked doves beneath each smiling year.
A tongue of music peels; afterwards grass-burst through tombs at
        sundown – twice
'Towards' our seraph sweethearts: who always wore deathshead
        rings on brown centre fingers.
But beware: man-snarl of irises on dewlapped graves: all Christ's
        long tears.

THE VAN POOL

Fair dooze and red rims eye. The World
Whose sparing goddam curses curled
To fix like tea on blunt Glamorgan
In the shadowed ball of bran.

Fair weather horse sense to tamed amuser
Whose pity chimnies land in cruiser
The blue-black day from Saxon grey
A view of spat and permanent way.

Vinegars swallow filleted ha – chaps
And pretzels obey raw ginger nips
How then avoid red-rim *eyes*?
        Oh my!
Lord don't hide our sky-wished dyes.

LAUGHARNE PASTORAL

The concrete under gale, the field, the pattern
All vanish: stark nightmares begin:
The lovesick slave lurks behind what's certain,
At home a heavy tramp walks to the barn.

Harlequins: the layers of dreams, unfurled
The people who go to make my world,
The circling valley swarms with ghosts,
Explosions in the head, the first, the worst.

Coracles catching Aeriel's birdsong
Shouldered into inns where men belong!
Salmon moving up weir: ducks over loam,
Drakes: against the delicate lace of foam!

But the landscape that child built
Wells up through mountain silt,
The simple words of my folk
Now break philosophies like yolk.

Farm-boys who sat on iron roller
After school, inherit frights no smaller.
Tripped up: a single myth, maybe – a Fool's:
The nation's brown-bottomed river-pools!

'SHIFT'

(To P.C.S.B.)

Now fighting birds fly south across tall seas
Leave salt of fields-in-air and humming wires
Migrate along trade-routes with swimmer's ease
Knowing what way is safe when the old guide tires.

The double wingbeat midair calling us
(Like male emperor moth) or ancient omen
Of black owl crying mere murder without fuss
Is proved bird killed like any virile human.

This shows their aim uncharted, their home lost
All faith in early nesting – bare despair.
All hope of landing, ship or some spirit protest
Just betrays action in the family elsewhere.

POEM

Bodied in darkness Pandora still attracts,
Lolls, until somebody comes 'home', needs her,
Stock exchange gallant or quaint smiling drifter
On fringe of society – Byron-hard blackness

Experienced infidels greedy ox-lovers
Crooked thunderbolts in sucking guest-chambers
Pokerhot letters endless whited dollshouse worlds
Alluring monstrous like pantheress at crossroads
Procrastination penned-in flowers unfurled
– That radiance favourite of the setting sun!
Ground slips whimsy under feet near her abode

Temptation: balanced as ruinous raffish confession
Rains: towards man's end – a whirlpool question
For adolescent shame one watched Atlantic's bore
In a lifting shack beside a peat furze fire ...

O blue flame o servility
              (a mauve blouse
Holding maddening hunter hearts circlewise).

Now know thyself and humbly forgive the feared
Gold-satire visions of a buried sleeping bard.

If Pandora attracts; not a word be spoken.
Let magic stress facts when truces are broken.

THE VAN POOL: TICHRIG

The day, comforting, warm on the ridge, hurried
By me, lying on grass, with a dog licking my face,
Bathed in a basin by the climbing sun; all clear;
No fade, where the shallow river ran dry
Leaving fish trapped in pools near lace curtained farms
– Boy angler's Lovely Day, – a labourer on step ladder echoed
Blindly over October cooking apples, all equals in plumpness.
Opposite, on a bloodless bank, Llansadwrn slept unattacked
As all pretty hamlets should; on our home side,
Garn Goch: broad backed, a single Roman wall, built up
To meet one last leafy hedge at boundary gate
Named by these red ferns' rusty stare and everyday coloured
Except for the patches scythed out for bedding.
Each wing tilt meadow, a little absurd for certain
Bad lads, roughly seven, now lined up at village square.
Inimitable geese growing in clumps on the common
All knowing the black iron bridge is wire netted!
Like tall small holders' sheep that never troubled leet courts
Whose grazing rights uncoil, whose homagers burn the upper hill-
        side region gorse.
..... O mewing gull flapping idly above roof slates and cottages
Showing pink through the trees showing white
As on this mountain turf I lie.

Noiseless, Towy winds grandly through the land, no flood below,
No tuneful nightingale charms the forest with her tale
Ah! the Mabinogion tales of Wales!
(When will the landskip tire the view?) seven humpy crows across a
        plain
Suddenly peopled with bob-whales of hambone brightness.
Stroke a collie's fine-fleshed leg for the glimpse would repay an
        insurance man.
Why are there wheels ? O why ? Why does this brown road
These cart rucks bring back old discontents leading
Over the Black Mountain in black nights ?
We never by each other's side
Even though the road is edged with whitest stones
O why am I the victim of a widened horizon
A summer cipher aching and living after reading

Social service reports (heirs of quiet sun warmed beings)
Murmuring deep. O why? O why? Love's humours pale by ghastly
       tumours.
Who follow near groggy hollows while music fills our sky.
For pith, fruit, stones, for ghosts of a pickled hill
The seeming everlasting light, vibratory, undulating
Cut out of this valley, or felt
For the illusion and the natural pleasure
I wish you could have been here too, Eirlys,
To have it painted on canvas for good
You, only you, could have caught that riddle
That blue afternoon's farness.

RIVER SAWDDE

When I step thimble heeled at an end of day
Sound of water Sawdde water pricks my ear,
A spreading dynamo sheer over all stone
Except for the round ribbed ones to wash it by.

Never trunk of tree on a sunken 'twmpath'
Met man or bill or hedging glove as I was there,
No smell no taste no speaking cold by people with a bell
In the finished disc of moon could but resemble

The next line open in wind tremble, heart whole being
Up the hillside moving as if telltale fingers
Were uncoffined at some thread; a mascot falls in love.

What it is to have water running near one's own house
With eels in it – alone – real – a one-syllabled water language.
Those town fellows have borrowed beetles in their shoes!

SONG

Here I am under a tree in the shade
Wondering how G.P. bombs are made

With whiskey I'm dosing the lambs to sleep
Gentle as a dog after laden sheep

Take a penny bus ride from the tube
See the beautiful flat where they're sucking a jube

The planes in the sky are as clean as a shilling
Both talk like a parrot when Vickers are shelling

'Scorpiones Pungunt' and its remarkable record
Assemble the parts, don't look at the blackboard

Now steel is as scarce as Harrow Boys
Phosgene and thermite eat up the public monies

O with chalk with instructors and boys in twill
And .303 guns they are teaching to kill.

RUMOUR ROUND THE FARMYARD

Mealtimes crack crazy and the hooting horn
Calls you hillbound in the broth, grafting
Supplanting the dewy outing, the delta café,
You are at gander guard, toads hop across the road.

Loose box heifers improve and fast on ozone grass
The twin calves suck together; but paw, for 'decline'
Is baaaed; hurry; remove; to the knackers yard
In a tarpaulin lorry; or mortgaged

Through a dug orchard hole if phoneless peasant
(Beasts fed at long ends of hired work)
Think of Black Fever as you shut the gate
Behind you driving milch herds to millstreams.

Reclaim the boned slope of gorse of bracken
Sweep with cool eyes hayseeds over barn's
Concrete; cakes the scouring cows; hen-coops;
Await loads like gambos paint shaved in the sun.

A hooting horn, a hobbled ass on common; horsedung
Brushed from paving stones, the chippings to the green.
Against the nameplate, hung high, no number.
Your sole alibi in the turn-ups of your pants.

WELSH SONG

Emotion's onlooker
Knitting of jig-saws
The copper interior
At the Influenza Hour
The whole family home at one o'clock
A White Lady
And a tail-less sow
Whittling away Time's enchanted bell.

FAME

Complete strangers arrive in cars at three:
Dressed in country tweeds, they talk of Journey,

Lunch, the Usk, the black shadow under the Vans,
The methodist valley; out of hovel-clustered commons

Children, sun-pennies given and the charm-smiles lost.
Drive Em Away needs wrinkles on perfect host.

Farm-questions shiver before our kitchen fire.
Stapledon? and so do I in downstairs terror.

How well those *different* people mix with these!
Bunkum regrets at small-talk, 'who likes cheese?'

If Lindberg is symbol, it's a cult of failures.
And Walcs is hard on that, mine heart, the champ's, yours.

Point out *the I*, conventional phenomena.
The mythic lake; help over stile for Brenda!

Here castle; one wife confessed pregnancy.
Quotes a neat line by a contemporary.

Hurries for early tea. They toast the hot-cross buns.
And depart like friends with brand-new double puns.

Where. The sherry party at the County Club?
They never ask me back. That's the last rub.

CHESSMAN ASSOCIATIONS

Idly scratching his name with a diamond ring
Across the woolly pane our Shelley sings:
Enough to keep breast of heiress burning.

Wordsworth, late pilgrim, stands on the bridge, ponders.
As trio pour wishes into pebbly Dee, wonder
'Were the Ladies ladies?' by lakeside and under.

Far from the all bordering metaphysic
Smart Hebrew scholars reason for bee tunics,
Their souls elevated by cathedral music.

More risky sprees faint back through milky tramways –
Rimbaud and Charleville, Savage in goal, rays always;

Landor lays £70,000 on dreams and estate.
Our modern monk bothered at 'forehead' couldn't sweat.

CINQUE PORTS

Here in a bell-tent in a half-way field near Dover
I have found myself resolved of race contradictions
And all regimentation, like the O most reassured lover   ·
Of a year ago, cast in a free world's imperfections!

Now peace is an ambush; the soldier alone mounts guard:
Thus we nine posted to a lonely site on a farm
Are a new war's inheritance exploring one's thoughts, reward
For our child's memory persistent as Dunsany's latest alarm.

By day we helped old Hambrook harvest corn
Being sons of good hunting yeomen in Romney Marsh
The whole detachment maintained a legacy inborn:
And still lit up hostile planes in nights bad and harsh.
(Yes, the farmer treated us like one of the family...)

Opposite, in fours, their flaming onions cross our sky,
Calais; Boulogne; the apparent kiss of Jerry beams on cloud,
Friend remarkably unhurt in bombed convoy out at sea,
But heartening flashes, fires there, expose our Blenheims' work,
         aloud.

Coming off guard after the official hours of darkness
A stack burns merrily before threshing against the dawn,
The neighbourly habits of to-be-shelled cowlike shapes the farm-
         house,
Sunrise, code-words, anti-gas; section officer on Invasion.

Wash and shave in the shippon, the present of eggs and milk,
         between
I ponder Empson's villanelle, cobwebs, magnetic land-mines. Sad?
Robot weather balloons like buzzing thermos transmitting wounds
     the shot-down 'shame' Dornier 17
One's safest in a bombhole, beyond majors, gunpits, whines,

         'Good fun? Ah, what a lad!'
And 'ubique quo fas et gloria ducunt' a Lotus ad!

MANLY AND ELIZABETHAN

(to dissolve Ten Neo-Georgians)

We are not of that spawn:
We who have seen No-Dawn
Painted by a generation
(Now commanding less veneration)
Whose symbol was Red Rose:
Hardly an adult pose!

RIDICULOUS WRENCH

Now like old Ruthven I must remember
Those days of a tragic late September
When I hung my scythe on an oaktree branch
Talking fears to neighbours over the hedge;
Or maybe digging graves for two dead ewes;
And hurried back home for an early lunch,
Across ten fields across windy reeds and wire
Dough-crocks on floor and on settle near fire
For the sparkless pulse of a year on edge:
Our troubled twice-reserved one o'clock news.

POEM TO BILL EMPSON

Death is too personal: it claims tranquillity;
      The desire for the exquisite pressure
            of the bee fails one.
Near deaths are the bulls before reveille.
      A formation of sixty-plus
                  like
      dive-bombers seem friendly as cloud-hoppers
Reveal disquieting frivolity,
Beads of despair on the brow
            (Quean Knave is always lack of feeling)
            while heart in strained argosy ticks over
            with its wild message.
Who know what it is to have job detailed to one
Unpleasant in course, who have seen schoolchildren
            not those   given boots.

It's here our altruism dies too
            – Cynics pointing the way in well-wearing Sensate
            epoch.

No, it doesn't quite fit in;
            death is too personal altogether.

      Iceland,
                  Singapore and the Near East
                  are certain hazy abstractions.

Killing is automatic;
machines are daily marvels
      still capable of impersonality to the remote
conscripts who will fire at one another nevertheless.
      But will the rulers escape scot-free this time?
      these youths seem innocent and are prepared
            to bear the overwhelmingness of fresh spilt blood,
      vote for no fleshy compensation,
      for only the lucky will dine on worse postwar afters,
      will be honest with the honey demands
            underlying women's irritations,
      And think on sleepless nights in barrack-room beds.
      When they were of good cheer,

no heirs of martyred breath, these
Bathed in the glorious mush of visions, gold and dreams
the young gunner's battle-dress against rich old men's resentment.
Or from the Red spouting destructively in our poor boy ranks
That mars potential infra-red, which might turn all sky's blue?

THE FOX

One hundred yards from the summit when the bells
Of hillside churches were inviting us to worship,
And the unspent splendour of a July sun
Drew us to the mountains – there suddenly,
On unsuspecting foot with quiet trot,
He made pathways of rare wonder before us;
We without moving, withheld our breath
Paralysed for the instant; like a trinity of statues
Stood, while he in the middle of a careless step
Himself stood dazed as well, and above
His one hesitant foot the two fixed flames
Of his eyes upon us. Then without haste or fear
His furry redness slipped over the ridge;
It happened, vanished, like a shooting star.

Translated from the Welsh of R. Williams Parry

SHEEP: GWYNFE

Slack falls, the vital heat, the healthy cheviots
Bought at Miller's draft sale – great gangs wedged in there
Look for rising smoke lifetime's curly blacking,
Wiping their feet on ferns; astride, after rugger collaring –
Leg well gripped in, then, only them lifted on haunches.
How the parings flew away from my penknife!
I had to get down on one knee for the front lot.

And flame on water; fingertips shrunken; nails blue. Mankind's
Shriek at crusted Stockholm backs at maggot cheats.
Long tails sheared; highland blood easy in red paint pools.
The butting dog linked in the barn, old veteran; a bantam pecks
At the big morning fowls' corn leavings; the yard's a little
Smeared with fluid; last scalloped ear, near mad, the mottled face
Stood up on vetted feet; purse-up, the fist eyed mating ram
A neighbour's lamb as well, the red marking brick
Had crumbled away. I counted fifty-eight into the field.

THE COCK PHEASANT

Because your multicoloured feathers are
Like autumn on your sleek bosom,
And every wealthy colour that ever was
Goes and comes as far as your back,
Let the law keep you from injury;
I, for my part, cannot wish you harm.

Because of the proud clatter of your beak
And your haughty gaze at his lordship's territory
Tonight I would desire to have your flesh
A roasted delicacy on my table;
And live grossly for that bit of time
On one who battened on the fat of the land.

Translated from the Welsh of R. Williams Parry

TRIMMING HEDGES

With this sickle (symbol or no) in hand
Made of (to repeat) hand forged Sheffield steel
I recollect stone walls Roman here
Doubling through Cotswolds:
And grindstone in rickyard off an officer's farmhouse
On our way to the Seats of Learning ho
Once M.G.-tourer, Ross-on-Wye, etcetera

Past those poets' villages, Aldestrop and Granchester
'Oh why farmers trim their hedges is Botany and that'
Persists; a midget Christmas Tree televised
at Alexandra Palace toy horticultural-certificated image,
the hawthorn hedge of Cae Fair whisked off round
remember bending-over stiffness the signal boundary
like the middle of a shifting river

With upright-slanting ladder trim holly bush into cuckoo shape?
no fal-lals here – a bull looks through a hole in ecstasy
at the vista down between new twisting hedges
turning so cars can pass at expense of animal shelter
right down to the clinkered smithy.

Cut, sweep up, yes burn these tall expensive feeders!
(Betty Isaac galloping hard on the loose stone road;)
All lateral buds: an equal mass! the roadman will do the rest;
Our neighbours peaceful sharing the muddied cattle-pool
A continent of broken promises need revised counter-espionage
and all the time the anarchist sing Brother Brother

THE LIFE OF MAN

Man's life, like any weaver's shuttle, flies,
Or, like the morning rose, withers and dies,
Or, like a ministry, it quickly finishes,
Or, like a bubble, merely vanishes.

Or, like a candle, it each minute wastes,
Or, like a long ship under sail, now hastes,
Or, like a post-boy, gallops horribly,
Or, like the shadow of a cloud, goes by.

Weak are our houses, and strong the foe,
Short is our time, for sure the end is woe;
But as the hour of death's uncertain still,
Let us be ready, come he, when he will.

Translated from *The Welshman's Candle* of Y Ficer Rhys
Prichard (1579-1644)

IN MEMORIAM

Soldier

He gave his strength and his comeliness – for his country,
For the hearths of peace:
All you, his contemporaries, grieve!
A well formed lad is quiet dust.

Sailor

Bashful Tom, so warmhearted – who stays
Long in the ocean-deeps:
How cold is the dying at this hour
Under the water's current, under the wave's brine.

O marvellous undisturbed multitude – the dead
And the seaweed intermingled!
The pearl's parlour, the fishes' acre
Illuminating Education's grave.

Translated from the Welsh of R. Williams Parry

DEATH OF A HURRICANE PILOT

Only this morning he strode in slippers and sweater
Across to the Naafi for coffee and a bun.
And the keepfit sun duly paced this favourite
Like a Greek god.
The English hamlets he rediscovered during his
Periodic short-leaves will know him no more.
The inn signboards shifting lightly, his shotgun,
The spinneys releasing their ominous partridge.

Dinner time. We left our sweets on the plate unfinished,
And our hearts raced upwards to a zooming gleam.
A plane diving vertically, then the long second
Suspense, hits the ground CRASH
And the whispered prayer was a shout.
A column of unseen smoke honours the dell and
The fir trees hide more than gipsy's hand on warning common:
Two are detailed. Waddelove and I set off on Army bikes with rifles
Search high and low for over an hour, past the trip-wire wood:
We found the wreckage at last, at two, three miles away
Burning steadily, with the belts of ammo in the wings
      exploding with little whoofs
                        But
Too late: the pilot dead inside.
An R.A.F. officer soon came but interrogated nothing,
More concerned with the marvellous stress of aluminium
Gee what stress they take – wizard workmanship
And the mottled rubber from the self-sealing
      (none for him)
The cockpit hidden below the fume-laden ten foot hole –
An arc of armour plating on the side of this grave.
A small crowd gathered: young Buffs; then some Green Howards
Called at the tabled farm for bedding-straw for palliasses.

But nothing to identify this once-tearing glory of the estuary sky
Except Hurricane type plate with a serial number
And 'Repair' scribbled in pencil on the left wing – feeding tubes.
We searched desperately for a gun or a number: too hot.
With bleeding hands, faint from the killing fumes and human

Grease perhaps. For us soldiers merely another digging job.
Children, ghastly souvenir hunters, forty yards away kick the skull,
Imply life's a racket, turning over his scalp with a pointer-ing kick
Poor auburn hair and scatter-brained scattered brains, O
Whole scalp attached to a Comper Piccadilly helmet
O Science O beastly laws of relative comparison.
     hair waving in the breeze
      hair like yours Charlie
        like yours Sir
    among sprayed bits of fuselage
     marked in the grass

II

Some woman will receive the fatal wire tomorrow
A son or young husband cut off in his prime. Aged sorrow
Will reign within the walls of a double heart
And the experienced writer will reap his professional part
With a prim or cultivated poise, the formal touch. In *The Times*.
Some Pole perhaps will grace the death-fed green of Kent in swim-
    ming dare from a planet's blind-spot

And a map-reference will be given phonetically over the radio
    telephony set by a sergeant
Hurricane – Smersole Farm – Swingfield – field N.E. from farm
    buildings
Field behind stack.

It brought back the weeks I chased death's pre-war image high over
    Leicestershire.

A brasshat arrives.
    Dreaming like a Brigadier
(At Sandhurst with Tiger Gort in '06)
Of cavalry charges with sabres, cold steel, Hore Belisha
And other terrible devices for polishing off the Huns.
But the winsome infantry of his imagination are as obsolete as
Were the fine Polish horse-guards
    And he is old – a golfhouse drunk.

The Relief. Thank God. Another digging party with a
          sack (why not an air-raid 'dust-bin').
I refuse to reconcile anything for our serious-minded public.
Except the words of command of the brute old-style sergeant
          of the Queen's Westminsters. Two lads fainted straight off.

They mount guard at dusk. It wasn't a pretty sight dear lady.
It was war, bare war, nightmare to me still, callous as hell ... his
          genitals like boxing gloves.   But
Are brave spirits like his less valuable to you for this blotched
          ending?
Blond, feather-brained, dull, smoker of cigars,

Driving everywhere in high-powered cars,
This week-end pilot died for Something, that's sufficient.
Twice shot through the heart – 'Cassandra' of the *Mirror* under-
          stood.

Trees on the mellowed parkland will give their benediction.

LLANGADOG COMMON

The dialect of leaden sky
hoes rootcrops in harnessed soils,
a Corot highlight on the sty
– background ricks sleep in slow coils.

In the pluperfect mix of haze
right for Grade A of suburbs,
ten gallon T.T. friesians doze
on Bibby's mart-sold cud herbs.

Here is no baby crêche to bomb
that muckheaps masculine towns,
nor meadows drugged from hero tombs
bullet-drawn as ballots drown.

Its nerve is an implanted hold,
pony-jolt of floats and churns;
who shift a sun to earn rent's gold,
solve no crises by trade returns.

STONE

I heard that an ancient stone in Gower
Served as memorial to a famous warhorse.
After Crimea his master rode on him
Round these grounds.
O later on a journalist found *The* Celtic Cross
Carved by a timeless sculptor out of sandstone
– A knot of designs like photos in prisons
Pretended no personal pattern
As it balanced in open weather.
By this column by five other blocks and slabs
The death of a prince is recorded,
And though the nag merited the Latin
Of eaten signs on interlace tombstone
We can only dismiss them as suckling scars.
Such grieving winds once rocked our ageing cradle!
But to ourselves the pillar on mound is a fad
– A surrealist Stonehenge
Not quarried for a native circle.
Some say it was a vision.
Some in order to improve the view.

FLASHBACKS

Where I sleep now in a high attic is
The Prussian echo, blood in parenthesis.

London – the swollen heart, the island's face,
Breeding hope in each sorry refugee race.

Meanwhile the image, the West's inheritance,
Dumb ancestors punctuating a coloured dance.

Time lost on chess; an air base where I farmed;
Have declined Hamlet's seven corpses; I wasn't armed.

There: I fought the elements; society:
I was the Man of Courage in humility.

A Sea-Eagle; Chester's calm; a hymning room,
I didn't want others involved in my doom.

Visions at dawn from a boat (Pre-Roman)
Ink-cloud-hung-over, off the Isle of Man.

I weep. I know we play a tragic role.
A man part of the weather, heart-beat at Pole.

But here I am the lighthearted man: The Celt.
Queering my pitch, a grievance – O world-felt.

AIR RAID ON EAST COAST

In mist my enemy dodged between balloon barrage cables
knowingly or unknowingly
unafraid of running into a quick wire death,
the mist seemed foam to him.
In mist we saw him come
Dornier 215
We traversed – using square open sights
a sitting target
machine-gunning our netted gunsite
taking his time oh going so slowly
the pilot had time almost to get out of his plane
and shake hands with us.

all the 'immature' instrument numbers ducked
or took cover or
ran down into command post
from the German airman's banking wizardry.
fanatic 'bravery'
machine-gunning guncrews
at 50 feet.

On loading tray – fuse 1.25, three shells out
one in fuse-setter
exposed
waiting for Gun control or Fire 'order'
but one Lewis gunner ripped his belly
turned him off
and was later duly escorted to an orderly room
for disobeying an order!
we wiseguys didn't
mutinous bands
experienced in lack of leadership and
5th column initiative.

now a Heinkel follows
and yet another low-flying Dornier
same again
repeat performance
Stand Easy Outside Emplacement.

Oh what a happy band!
We curse our dog-ends, five Woodbines gone
spoilt in the wet
ask if anyone's hurt
condole with our 19-year-old M.M. over
his first time of non-firing.
Nearly didn't see you this week-end mam.
Don't be a Dick.
Oh browned-off comrades!

Sergeant said: Get tin hats on –
he walking without one himself
fondling his coldmeat ticket
making a mortuary joke
about stiffs 'So much dead meat'
but in between the Take Posts
rather too much nervous joking perhaps
laughter of excitement
of this daily carnal tussle with death
Identities unchanged, however
sensibilities still speak in Army language
I remembered an unfriendly death
38 slugs in one back
aerodromes dive-bombed Dover comrades
Welsh underlings like me!
the price of glory 4-inches in the guts and a camera.
un-cased in

>   high up on tray seeing what's going on
>   like a lone rider
>   it'll always be glory pope

the eyes of consciousness doubtless
          show not quite so blue and frank
those white tracers from his blister-gun
          were unexpected
blast circling targets!

an eye or an arm or a leg
mowed down in the back
          slugs fall at feet of gun
          ricochetting from concrete.

Looks like my funeral way we're carrying on
nobody to say a prayer over me
only the thin track of blood donors.

Here we'd be
dozens of ill-advised casualties
'But I like bombs flying around in Bromley
Queer – it makes the girls more loving.'

Yes, here we'd be
with bullets playing up our backs
with a handle in hand clutching a high tree
waiting for a Hurricane to take us to Heaven
still waiting to pull through the Pias Aba!

48 HOURS AT TENBY

Blue sparkle of sea rounding the harbour
Quay Alley opening on to two beaches
And blue, deep blue the bay over the sand
Following the vague indeterminate coastline
Green shadow of scaly waves on reddening sails
Airplanes banking overhead patrolling as far down as Worm's Head
Porpoises leaping near bathers in the calm oiled patches
And a little ship tied up at the pier
The island-green is monk deserted no other than Caldy
So pleasant after the eyesore rock called St. Catherine's Fort
A few marines and a dribble of a crack county regiment take it easy
... The refreshment bars on the shore might serve as orderly rooms
While cluttered ramshackle hotels with a sea-view cost the lucky a
       fortune
Grey men in flannels with Eton ties the genteel old and
Coffee-drinking newly marrieds with soluble baby napkins

Sun takes away the cares of morning and journey
Soft sand trickles through fingers and palms
Of those who feel awkward being still not free in mind
Sun does us good idling on the galloped sands
Tires us out before teatime.

The 'Welsh' Gift Shop sells reproductions of
Paul Nash, Matisse, Van Gogh, a country-life series,
buckets and spades, has a tabby cat in the window
And the houses in South Parade remind us of
Augustus John, Nina Hamnett, and Herbert M. Vaughan
who is known to speak up on the town council.

ALARM ALARM

I remember vapour-trails over Gillingham ... wavy
And the monument to the builder of the Japanese navy
And oil burning in black columns down Thameshaven way;
Queer happenings on Gravesend range; Croydon's day.

Detling divebombed – and Hawkinge – we got two;
I saw convoys screaming up the Channel's blue.
Connect dodged shells a lamp's smashed splendour with
A boy's M.M. earned defending Martlesham Heath.

A plotting board with one-five-o hostile;
The Italian raid; patrolling the beaches, Deal,
Oxney, Shakespeare Cliff and the invasion warning
From pier-extension to Dover Court, Felixstowe in Spring!

Joking and blood in a Nissen hut in South Ronaldsay.
The Flow: trips in a drifter to bird-splashed Hoy.
The *Prince of Wales* through an OSDEF telescope;
The leave-boat: a crofter snuffling his stony-crop hope.

All this I remember and more oh much more.
Digging planes King's Bench Walk The 'Temple' burning
But nothing nothing that I can compare
To love like a bell through Yarmouth flying!

ROOM WITH A VIEW

An oil-lamp flickers in my room of ashes;
A pair of rooks fly down the estuary;
Our dreams are more wroughtiron evening-washes
On poems that spell to me bad history.

So before the landscape folds itself away in shade
Where song-filled chapels fail each brilliant ode
And trippers come as refugees in caravan and shed
Let's plan our simple life, collect sticks in the wood.

What are our bootless cries past Castle, shell and shale
But triads for sandman cursing The Modern Age.
Humanity will always lick boots or drown in ale:
Go over seagrass, crablike, release canary in cage.

Walk like dog-gut postman, at best like an elm.
Know the museum scout for a dear old fool.
And crash through symbols as ill exciting school
Else newspaper lies, then, for these Celts' life-giving balm.

Llanstephan

WAR MEMORIAL

O monument of a father's and mother's grief!
    You, foremost throughout many lifetimes,
Teach a way with intense remembering
Of the rent of losing lads.

Translated from the Welsh of R. Williams Parry

HIS FATHER'S SON

Last year with the rise of the tide he took himself away
   Over the rough waves;
For his country he gave his oath,
   Over sea he turned to die.

This year he merits the calm of his gentle self;
   In that absent spot in tranquillity,
As on the earth's bed his dust spends
   The Christmas of his serenity.

Translated from the Welsh of R. Williams Parry

SOLDIER FROM MERIONETH

Near his breast a river runs, under talking
    Cheerfully as it goes by;
He does not listen, he says nothing –
    Under the clay he does not hear.

But Cefnddwysarn soil on him, was spread
    Very tenderly over him;
And the birds will come to him
    To tread about his grave.

Translated from the Welsh of R. Williams Parry

INCORRUPTIBLE

Before long this old body will be
        Meat for the fervent insects,
And the coffin plate and its glittering
        Trimmings alive with rust.

A sun will rise above the Vale of Towy
        Like a piece of God's Capital,
No vermin will be able to reach it,
        And rust shall not violate its colour.

Translated from the Welsh of D. Gwenallt Jones

THE SOLDIER'S PLAINT

Happy in daylight's handhold,
Puce shaded lips against tozing perfume,
My love and I wandered secretly
From restaurant back to a rug in a flat.
Then onto beerhouses; a negro afternoon club.
Past alleys, street markets, city lusts we steered,
Yet hungering privately ourselves,
As lovers have hungered before.
For, mythlike we seemed to live by pure guesswork then.
But corresponding emotions in a cinema
Showed love was a matter of money,
And now I, body and spirit, face a sky's death alone.

POEM OF ASKING

For James Findlay Hendry

Meanwhile hours wasted on the pyramids of to-day
– Between tears locked by angels in the age of bubbles;
Poring over black occult books like a coloured fly
While only Gradual Change binds ginger groups voluble.

Sunbeams hermetically sealed by the Coalowners' story
– Horror of sermon paper to automaton thirst
That the Robin Hood crucible strangles five fold spray
No deed magnate's blood crime is tapped by a nightly ghost.

Almost the centuries' shell of pain is sensed intense
In the soiled stop-days to esoteric decorums
And vain through holes in headlong bohemian colonies
Off-band fakir morose Magi but for paupers' Lent extremes.

Alone shopkeepers lie confused like heaven's joker.
Mischief's landlord draws partitions up to a tie-beam;
Then pulleys beds to a cold bath under a trap-door.
All 'highbrows' lost in the motions of one Arabian dream.

THE CURLEW

Your call is heard midday
Like a finevoiced flute above the moor;
Like a hidden shepherd's whistling
Your call is heard midnight;
Until is heard, when your note deepens,
The barking of your invisible dogs.

Your charge the bald tedious clouds,
Your willing dogs the four winds are
Who drive in folds your moist flocks
To scatter them a second time on their mission
Free in restless impulse without bleating
Along the level summer pastures of heaven.

Translated from the Welsh of R. Williams Parry

A SAILOR'S EPITAPH

Here is a sailor's grave – far out of reach
   Of the sea's severe thunder;
He is brought at last to a harbour
Where no wave is on the face of the water.

Translated from the Welsh of Tudno

SOLITUDE

Wind on sea and sun on mountain,
Grey stones instead of trees,
And gulls instead of men;
O God! why doesn't my heart break?

Anonymous *penillion* translated from the Welsh

THE STONE

On the sea shore there is a flat rock,
Where I once spoke a word with my love;
About it the wild thyme grows
And a few sprigs of rosemary.

Anonymous *penillion* translated from the Welsh

INSCRIPTION FOR A GIRL'S GRAVE

To the gentle give a resting-place – in cold March,
    In the torrent of winter;
Put a white complexion under the veil of ice,
Put tenderness beneath snow.

Translated from the Welsh of R. Williams Parry

ENGLYN: SNOWDONIA

The lakes – green – still – are sleeping
    In a shelter of mountain,
And the resplendent sunshine draws
On a sheet of water the day's image.

Translated from the Welsh of Gwilym Cowlyd

THE BATTLE OF THE CAMBRIANS
AND THE MICE

... a certain Taffy, *cui Wallia numquam aequalem peperit*
Cambromyomachia by Edward Holdsworth (1709).

After the great wits vexed in council hall,
Taffy, a tall smith, speaks of mechanic cunning
Among applause. Minerva's help; a thing for mouse.
Destroy the monstrous plague that ate our cheese whole.

The trap is made – *so*: the toasted cheese!
The simple mouse runs forward to a room.
The cat is summoned; the door opened.
The prisoner come to a thief's ancient doom.

Leeks and onions and garlic – planted.
The echoing hills of Plinlimon cross and recross
As far as the Wye – joyful, unconquered by Caesar.
Supper for ploughman; for the rich a third course.

Goats and beards and wars and regiments.
Goat-bearded features, a goat in a regiment.
Augustus John bearded throughout 'The Great War'.
The long pedigree an old language, 'Rabbit' – and Taffy no more!

SECULAR MYSTIQUE

While the purring lorry climbed up hill
My beating heart stood still,
It might have been some dream on an iron will.

A tear from heaven
Then blocked my course star-driven,
Body falling through space through burning ovens.

Already Time hung in my hands
A morning clock, a siren towards those lands
Where soul and spirit are lost in painted sexless winds

Spelling delight in air – in earth – oh what
Is tragic is Braille, alone – or a dead cat,
Plane in lake, deaf and dumb signs, or a bat

Turning full on to our slow rolling eye
Fierce as enchanting *so*-fearing our quandary.
The reddening devil knows our very real love for the rockery.

DOG

Here at my feet the dog rampant
sad-eyed licks white-tipped paws
showing pink tongue momentarily
and then to push rat-burrowing nose forward.
Now his long body assumes a hunting shape
his wiry form glistens like light-shine on black hair
his long tail wags, he breathes gently to his haunches,
sighs; rolls over on the side of his belly
resting (it's night-time)
in the hungry shadows as when puppy lodged
forgets poor torn canker ear, distemper, worms
the sheep-half native
the other
heir of some heeling corgi of the
Pembrokeshire or Cardigan hills.

POEM ON BEING INVALIDED OUT
OF THE ARMY

O then let brain fetch back its deep creative urge
– below or above normal
and wonder and exhilaration find
some evening quiet when all cares away
the mind is flushed and steadfast in its purpose
selective with a legislator's love:
heart beat clean like genius in a garret
making its Attic gift to an accepting world
irrigated by no fantasy of that old sad life
cut terrible accusing patterns in each headpiece
whose most real imagery gives some new impact
to our small bier and skeleton-bones, 'that' ghostly appearance
whose mask – or 'face' can flare within the dirty bag of skin:
and like medieval types the one-per-cent
out of an insignificant and fleeting art
live on the ruler's page – despised anonymous personalities,
admonished by the other half from whose callous sanity
the whole mad recognizing world is unanimous in enormous self-
       redemption.

FIRST PEACE CHRISTMAS

Nights full of music and of merry carols,
pleasant yarning till the early morning;
another Christmas – see the miracle again,
the old magic had not forsaken Wales!

The young men who were caught by gluttonous Death –
o tender be the sleep of their long exile:
grieve, my brothers, wherever you may be,
under dust of cities for ever ruined.

For the fear that mocked us before the battle,
was false. No one broke the warm intimacy of
the language of our fathers, of the careless laughter of children.
Thanks, comrades: sweet be your costly yearning.

Translated from the Welsh of Alun Llywelyn-Williams

EPITAPH

Here lies a war baby
In a masked farm,
That lived in the first-taste
Of Invasion alarm.

His faery Lady
And still-armed lake,
A vote in the wind,
A face made fake.

White heat of sun
Fans his dead bones,
Buried as gun noise
Under the redwood stones.

PROEM

(for Robert Herring)

As words and world
honour yourself
so let their heirs unfurled
awake love outside Self

if one's self glows
then all else follows!

FOR THE LATE LORD HOWARD DE WALDEN

I

Striding behind those iron gates in echoing Chirk
O ghost of great patrons! unfolding in Ceiriog's vales –
Awaken the native music of contemporary Wales!
A hero's armour for the modern pageant's work!

II

    Oh ye Foolish Cymry
He offers you a theatre out of his heart,
Wrote the first man of the world who understood words:
Despite a difficult heritage you played your part;
But Conformity triumphed and we're left with 'bards.'

MINISTRY OF INFORMATION: MALET STREET

For Cecil Day Lewis

With scissors and paste, the propaganda – points at will,
Redfaced advertising men plan how to sell the war;
The Yanks are laughing in the Lower Pleasure Bar;
And perhaps the Saga of the Killed is bloodier still.

LITERARY 'CONSERVATIVES'

Their patriotic words echo rusty perdition
In verse that falsifies a fine tradition:
While our hot Idealists, shot with lead,
Leave deathless poems – far better dead.

ON READING CERTAIN 'ANGLO-WELSH' LITERARY CRITICISM

Link up his name with Vaughan's –
And Shoni-Hoi's with Donne's:
– Like him you've novelised a thesis
And have not looked back since!

BARDIC CROWN BALLAD

(for D. H. I. Powell)

Together we crossed the frontier, you and I
Feet up, dozing slantwise in the train,
We saw the Flanders Plain high in the sky
Like old soldiers come to war again.

We talked of poets, painters and of Style
While pitying the white faces of the young,
Although you nearly missed us out at Lille,
Neither forgot the land from which we sprung.

We munched at odd hours, had lunch at one,
Then you went off to see the Monmouthshires,
The hanging Germans were basking in the sun,
Miles from the avenging Fusiliers.

Behind us Calais lay – joyless place to see
Whose very people lack the life we made,
Unlike our own unconquerable souls now free
From the heartburn of a bad decade.

And then the battle flamed in sweat and blood
Of heroes who'd come by the long track,
And we called on angels from where we stood
Climbing to guide us safely back.

But as in a dream the figures hover and enter
Like the S.S. man with his Schmeisser,
Beyond the flashes on the horizon centre
The flails flamethrowers and mineclearers.

We took it down, both you and I
And sent our dispatches off home,
One boot glued to mud like a fly,
Time glints like light for some.

And morning came in the Reichswald part
After chasing the crooked cross,
And we propped a stone under our heart
To ease the hours of loss.

The pine trees dripped on the bodies even,
I lay on the grass and thought of the Dead,
For many a man had been marked for heaven,
But I kept Despair at bay with the mad.

And by firelight in tavern and on inn bench
In days to come survivors will retell,
How men were good and great among the stench
And had bigger visions than those of Hell.

Yet I feel old and mourn my brothers
With wounds in stomach and heads bashed in,
Behind my eyes a pain stabs like sin
Praying silence when looking at each other.

VICTORIA LEAVE TRAIN

In the sixth year faces are as tense as ever,
Lit up in the crowded train on the return journey,
My Generation death-image-haunted as in a fever.

Homesickness sprawls on packs with a sad sleepy smile,
Red flashes of courage, echoes of fading adventures,
Bother the Midnight subconscious as mile on mile

A flush of correspondents sit like migrating swallows
Unaware of the mapped forest and the assembled shallows
Watching the beginning of one more trip to the End.

From the tossing, the lolling bodies of early morning
Lingering in files, from the assembled derisive sneer
Comes no sense of Identification and certainly no singing.

For them it's loudspeaker directions under the electric glare,
A second hard embarkation bereft of many a luckless friend.
Soldiers with families O who pities you as you were?

You boarded the Ship whose decks were swept, you slept
Outside cabins; or changed your money with sore heart,
Expecting to go every minute expecting the show to start.

Yet you never grumbled like a secondline draft
Back beyond A Echelon; so if there are saints aboard
Let them send up their complaints like a thunderclap to heaven.

And will the Soldier who brought back a model last week
Of a Spanish galleon as a present go to ship's deck forward
If he is aboard

Waiting, waiting, it is always waiting around
For something to happen, for the issue to be decided

Resigned – these are not glory-fed, have no illusions.
Remember the cinnamon dust of Normandy, their booby-trapped
        dead.
And they also know the despair of battles won

For only the Fortunate
will ever run the gauntlet of the queue's eager
questioning eyes at Victoria again.

ABERFAN: UNDER THE ARC LIGHTS

Ask what was normal in green nature and its pain:
Will rain undermine our homes and us again?
Ask those scrabbling garden-breakers, the mountain sheep
Where are the classroom's children? – and then weep.

O martyred town shorn of its crown of glory!
That dumpy matriarch scanning in our fury
For faces of first-borns in the two handed-bier;
All the elements of tragedy are here.

Waters of history still in midnight's deep
Drip in Ceridwen's cauldrons; rage eisteddfod, seep
Into the jagged stalactites of hearts' hours.
Crushed out of life like paper-petalled flowers.

Ask courting couples whose coats took dust off the tips;
And hand back to the heavens stars on the future lips;
Children conceived in mist whose playground it had made.
Blame breeds guilt with blind anger in its road.

The whole bare drama played out as it looms
To a world-shared audience in their evening room;
One human chain of rescue under arc-light glare.
All the elements of tragedy are here.

Unpublished Poems

ON REMAND

Sun comes gleaming
thru wall window
of ice-barred temple
     punishment enough

Brain-pixies play
outside blank street
of telescoped suburbia
     green envious eyes

Hopes from hopelessness
catapult ideas bereft
of beauty courage
     inhuman pals

Life-governor releases
one hardened thought
of inevitable reconviction
     x works

CONVERSATION IN THE BLACK-MARIA

Yes perhaps more grim than a mediaeval fortress
as you
draw up in your stuffy tender from the Old Bailey
seeing
the visiting magistrate on his weekly round in his Daimler
admiring
the prim lawns
and the borders between the V.D. hospital and the chapel.

Of course the Scrubs is for the better type of man
and first offenders
and there the 'screws' treat one decent in the 'reception'
list your
belongings while you bath and put on fumigated prison clothing
conduct you
thro' mirrored corridors to the B.I. hall;
hot cocoa
and six ounces bread:
then curfew
you make up your bed-board in your cell (or not
if hard labour)
a bell rings at five to eight.

Exercise or gym according to physique
next morning
quite like a public school – marksheets
eye-holes
what with anchored nostalgia, asphalt and
sirs
to warders, Chaplains, S.M.O. and Governor
When-do-you-go-ups from old lags intent on
Oakum mailbags

The pot-smells in the slop-out interval haunt
us war-babies
not yet settled down from twinges of claustrophobia:

But think of Latin America; 20 chained to a post
excrement-circles
and lowered buckets of water, loaf struggles within the radius
for here
you have a visit or a letter a month the tearful card reminds
in C 87 cell,
(...you speak thru glass and love-letters maybe suppressed
and sex).

(or should this poetic be:)
Want of tobacco was driving us mad
We thought the sermons and lecturers sad
the menu hung for the grub was bad
and canvas-shop hours always bored us lads
What was the use of us sending petitions
Knowing the governor's and Home Office hallucinations

If it's any help please remember the one-sixth remissions, please!
but don't pray
for here the sycophants lose no stripes, no privilege
in fact
Work as in a dream and leave as in a dream.

STABLELAMP AND BEDDING

This is the daily round of work
Byre to be swept with cane brush
Even on Sundays I can't shirk
One must get rid of the slush

Cowspiss slices ways to grating
Cesspool is pumped to a tank
Herculean is my greeting
Pushing barrows up the plank

Hone our shield knives on the whetstone
Cut the haymow in the barn
Pitchfork high loads piled to fern cones
– *These sons of the soil*, you learn

Chucked bundles fill mixed byng with feed
Cattle-licked like timbered mangers
Pastures monthly spread with liquid
Oil-cake tons cut calendars

From the sloping orchard field
To friesians Proo Proo is a call
And water meadows heifers yield
Now safe chained, twice looped, to stall.

Udders sluiced with flannel smacks
So grow Milk Bars from pap-pail
We six put on our milking smocks
Our hands drowned in pit pat of pail

Blood hot it streams down the ploughed cooler
And strains through gauze to churns
Gallons – all lined with foot ruler
And labelled lids are given turns

C.W.S. lorry picks up at the stand
By A.A. box dud tavern
Station sends most milk in the land
Our floats tied in its cavern

The United Dairies glass-lined tank
Is slipped out from the siding
The laden trolleys grunt and crank
The van. Shove, we, porters guiding!

Now heading for milking machines
Vet clips ears for register
Let's go easy – say – are there fines?
Farming's independent Mr

FOREIGN NEWS

Sozzled, the world's oyster, Laurie
Whose photo hangs in Fleet Street bars
Drinks with newshawks back from nondescript
Fronts in la rue Duphot. Dauphin and
Geisha girl throng threads through bloated press
Brains. Westward, the crow flies. Past night beneath
Pink eiderdown, beneath marine life
His courtesan, the fallen model
of seven capitals and him her
Plastered, explosives staccato planned
From halfway archipelagos elegant of
Verbiage clipped by his Dictator Book,
His doped Society Features.
Three – it is the Central European
Situation. Four – the Dalmatian
Coast. Five – the Rhine. Alarums barbwire
Thermite. She snores. So diligent night-jars.
Tomorrow he is fulfilled, days shorten,
Contracts are with human interest,
Tyro the splurges for illustrated *Meteors*.

TERCET AND A LYRIC INTERLUDE

Step over dung with peelings for a bull
hit me on the head with a mop my love
yes yes ma whistling three dozen dams

milk the friesian with hanging afterbirth-
dressing into a Heinz bottle
there's no one to take a turn for me
buy my Xmas pegs made with my own hand
washed on the baking heaven tree.

HANES GWAED IFANC Y TYWYDD

I, blood, beat in the elbow of a room,
Light on the nipple, gold turned onto glass
And look on ooze bookblue,
One saw a whale, the other arms to rest in
Gorau cam, cam cyntaf
Know that thus I build my luckless monument
of evil stones on-go the red red garn
oh hobble soul, the fear, the semen in the hand
not stars, not mud, no trappist heart I gave
Cas gŵr na châr ei wlad
who guide me slow to the falling museum of eyes
the holiday match of loony salute and wet
my shah trick riding at the show shadows
my in-grown polyp whips my in-grown sister's hair
sodden and virginal, soaked in hysteria
Gwell pwyll nag aur
its apogee in animal, noise and savoy chapped
ba-baaing below, perverse in inverted public
paced that swaying year the groan – oh the milk
in the stiffs and withdrawn, by spiralling buzz
beast hot it climbs the bell belly-round
and chooses to an ah and the seasalt mirror
Nid ar drot y mae cardota chwaith
but only
but only by this
by this notorious wind
the anne sponge of days
where the radnor railway loses
the hippospiny mis-en-scène
I, blood, beat in the elbow of a room
Dyfal donc a dyrr y garreg
Nid tân, heb eirias

VIOLENCE: WALES: 63-64

I

The bells of Llangendeirne
A tale tell of iron –
Folk from Glam's Swansea:
'Remember Aberdovey'

Is their stale toll.
So magistrates all,
Your writs won't yield,
One padlocked field

While the villager spies,
Their true enemies,
Clerks of a city,
Boring a sea.

United we stand,
While on other hand
Offer an acre
Or 2 *beyond* Rhandir-

mwyn and the Highwayman's
Own robber highwayman's
Uninhabited cave
as alternative.

So let engineer roam
With writ and hacksaw;
Not a single home
Without the law

Will drown in Shir Gâr.
So off in your car,
Make the other valley,
Run down our Towy

But save Gwendraeth Fach
And our village, *bach*;
Make Ruddy-deaf-aid
A sheepfold indeed.

II

In the farmhouse out West
Growing plays and bullrushes:
The *hwyl* has gone sour;
Bible-black's no longer best.

The *cawl* in the bowl,
Wooden-spooned from iron pot
By the heroine in love,
Buoyed by the party prowl and howl.

Violence: oh what mad career
For one so noble and very dear!
A girl can only translate, *translate*
And not betray a country's pathos.

Next week year again will flame
Violence; historical as reason,
More terrible, notable, recent:
Blame a flash of sun at noon.

Blame Llangefni: not a word
Was at eisteddfod spoken,
Only the old truce was broken;
Now the gelignite boys, The Sword.

The poets and men-of-letters
Are mostly behind it, with-it;
The laurelled Whitehall morals,
Inflexible at Aberystwyth.

In Merlin-land the locals say,
Blow, blow, don't squeeze it dry;
The Chief Constable's one of us;
Come, you can say that again.

A swig of punch from the dairy,
Gaiety before the long car-ride
Towards Liverpool's dogs unloosed:
Now the gelignite boys, The Sword.

Outside the house in the drive
Who poked the boarded window?
But this was a message long ago:
Dig, dig the lessons of our history.

Violence, the face in the mirror:
The inescapable horror,
Ultimate terror:
And ministerial error.

Destroy what are our assets,
Bosworth to Tonypandy riots;
Detonate the flowering Ethos,
Wake up the funereal North.

Notes

First and subsequent dates and places of publication are given for each poem, where relevant.

Poems from *The Van Pool & Other Poems*

The Prodigal Speaks
Furioso, vol. 1, no. 3, Spring 1940, p. 29; Now [Series 1], no. 2, June-July 1940, p. 5.
Rhys was born on 26 December 1913, at Llwynyrynn, a farmstead of Bethlehem, Carmarthenshire, to Morgan James Jones, a farmer, and his wife Hannah Margretta Jones. His name at registration of birth was William Ronald Rees Jones.
Ben Christmas and Dan Joshua: According to Census records, Daniel Joshua was born in 1887 and Benjamin Christmas in 1883. Certainly in 1911 they were local to Carmarthenshire.
Eirlys: Mary Elizabeth Eirlys are the given names of Rhys's younger sister, who died of croup on 5 April 1919 at the age of two, and is buried in the grounds of Bethlehem Chapel. The name Eirlys translates as 'Snowdrop'. Rhys's unpublished and incomplete poem 'Gwynfe' describes his memory of Eirlys's death and burial:
'The ministers at Llyn yr ynn, at chapel, graveside/ I cried and my aunts consoled me (one remains)'. (National Library of Wales Archive)

Poem on Being
Poetry, vol. 53, no. 4, 1939, p. 186.

The Good Shepherd
Life and Letters Today, vol. 19, no. 15, 1938, p. 54.

Interlude
Twentieth Century Verse, no. 14, December 1938, pp.126-27; *Modern Welsh Poetry*, 1944.
Their way to vans: the Carmarthenshire 'Vans', or mountains.
The lady, the lake, both sleeping: the first of several oblique references to the myth of the 'Lady in the Lake' at Llyn y Fan Fach ('The Van Pool'). See Introduction.

The Emigrants
Life and Letters Today, vol. 20, no. 16, December 1938, pp. 44-45.
Mencken: H.L Mencken (1880-1956), American journalist and critic.
Utica: U.S. city in New York State.
Brython: Briton; Celt.
Madog: legendary 12th Century Welsh prince who is reputed to have sailed to America and established a colony.
Ericson: Leif Ericson, Norse adventurer, fl. 11th century; *Eriks Saga* describes his voyage to the North American continent. Rhys's chronology

of alleged early European visitors to America is somewhat debatable.
Dai mon: with the sense of 'Dai, mate!'

Barddoniaeth
Twentieth Century Verse, no. 14, December 1938, p. 126.
Barddoniaeth: Welsh for 'poetry'.
(For J., D. and D.): For James, Dee, and David Hendry.
Allenbury's: a British make of baby feeder bottles. The name was presumably also attached to growth charts.
Musso: Vido Musso (1913-82), jazz saxophonist.

Poem for a Neighbour
Twentieth Century Verse, no. 3, April-May 1937, p. 46; *Modern Welsh Poetry*, 1944.
Molly: Rhys gave Lynette Roberts a copy of this poem shortly after they met. She recalls in her 'Notes for an Autobiography': 'His poems to me were very good. One, 'Boxing Day' ['The Prodigal Speaks'] and another about Molly with him in the field. I was a little jealous of Molly as I thought I only filled his thoughts. Then he wrote and said Molly was his pony!' Lynette Roberts, *Diaries, Letters and Recollections*, p. 206.
buckler: a small shield.
Tresaith: Tresaith is a small coastal village in Cardigan Bay.

Letter to Lord Beaverbrook
Seven, no. 7, Christmas 1939, p. 27.
Lord Beaverbrook's 'Empire Crusade' campaign for economic protectionism, largely publicized in his *Daily Express* newspaper in the early 1930s, had the support of many within the farming community.
mythical lake under Towy's source: the River Tywi flows from the Cambrian Mountains, past the hamlet of Bethlehem, and into Carmarthen Bay. The mythical lake and the cattle are once again redolent of the 'Lady in the Lake' story surrounding Llyn y Fan Fach.
bright halloo of Simon Lee: wistfully and playfully introduces the younger years of Wordsworth's pastoral huntsman.

Week-End in South Gower
Horizon, vol. 3, no. 14, February 1941, p. 150.
Pwlldu: a river flows to Pwlldu Bay on the Gower Peninsular, where it is damned up behind storm beaches. The area has several caves in which some Palaeolithic remains have been found. It is a region haunted by ghosts of the industrial and mythical pasts.
Pennard Castle: the ruins of the medieval castle overlook Three Cliffs Bay close to Pwlldu.

Spin
Twentieth Century Verse, no. 8, January-February 1938, n.p.
This is not the only poem by Rhys that describes pre-war flying school experience. See also 'Air Pageant', 'Rip Van Winkle', and 'Cross Country' for other examples.

Section from the Van Pool

Poems from the Forces, 1941.

Rhys married Lynette Roberts in Llansteffan in October 1939. This poem draws on memories of the occasion of their marriage, and the early months of married life in Llanybri. As such, it touches on areas of experience also recorded in Roberts's poems and diary entries of the same period.

Geraldis: Giraldus Cambrensis, the medieval Welsh historian and chronicler.

Plata estancia: in Roberts's 'Radio Talk on South American Poems' she recalls: 'During the interval that my father was General Manager for the Buenos Aires Western Railway and was contemplating buying an *estancia* in Mar del Plata, I sent him a sonnet supporting his opinion of administration and the beliefs which he held.' *Collected Poems*, p. 110.

Langain Road: the village of Llangain is close to Carmarthen.

strip-bath: compare Roberts's description in her diary entry for 7 March 1940: 'Keidrych (that is my husband) and I wash once a week: we boil a bucket of water, strip-tease exposing a small bare patch of flesh, we scrub the exposed part violently, then cover the part with wool, and immediately attack another part.' *Diaries, Letters and Recollections*, p. 9.

'pele': from Roberts's diary entry for 15 January 1940: 'We make our own "pele" and most rural villages still use this...We have used the clay brought up from Cwmcelyn and mixed one bucket of this with seven buckets of coal dust and a quantity of water...The mixture has a distinct binding quality and is always put on the fire damp.' *Diaries, Letters and Recollections*, p. 7.

Garn Goch

Poetry: a Magazine of Verse, vol. 53, no. 4, 1939, p. 187; *Poems from the Forces*, 1941.

Garn Goch: the red cairn, is the largest Iron Age hill-fort in Wales, and overlooks the hamlet of Bethlehem and the River Tywi.

pooled Van: once again an oblique reference to Llyn y Fan Fach and its legend.

Letter to my Wife

Poems from the Forces, 1941.

Rhys was called up to the army on 12 July 1940. His postings took him away from Roberts and Llanybri for months at a time.

White Cliffs: Rhys was stationed near Dover as an anti-aircraft gunner, where Roberts visited him in November 1940. She remembers the events in her 'Notes for an Autobiography': 'Letters fail to arrive from Keidrych. This was unusual as we have written to each other weekly. In the last he openly stated that he was taking a girl to the cinema and holding her hand. I was worried about the consequences, but admired his openness. I believed in being faithful to Keidrych and not kissing and taking hold of the hand of anyone else. He had been moved to the anti-aircraft guns in Dover. There they had shelling from the French coast as well as overhead bombing. I would go and see him... Something was wrong. Keidrych could not make love to me, he had got used to this other woman and their ways in the dark... I thought the best thing to do was to give him a tremendous kiss and I did this and he asked me to do it again.' *Diaries, Letters and Recollections*, pp. 216-18. Argentine warmth: Roberts was born in Buenos Aires of Welsh-descended parents.

Poem for a Green Envelope
The Van Pool, 1942.

Green Envelope: a standard army stationery issue to enable letters to be sent home, under an honour code, uncensored by unit officers. Such letters were liable to censor at a further stage of their journey.

pawls and cams and differentials: mechanical constituent parts of an anti-aircraft gun.

Deanna Durbin: famed Canadian singer and actress.

fuse-setter... tray... emplacement report: artillery terms.

OCTU: Officer Cadet Training Unit.

Jack Hulbert: a British film actor popular in the 1930s.

Lewis Gun: the Lewis automatic machine gun was used as an anti-aircraft gun throughout World War II.

'a dynamic equilibrium...': Rhys introduces a scientific phrase from the discourses of chemical reactions, biological systems, and thermodynamics.

Skinner's rare humour: possibly a reference to Reginald Denny's 1926 film *Skinner's Dress Suit*.

windlassing: in the sense, perhaps, of 'ensnaring'.

Nissen huts: huts made from corrugated iron with a concrete floor.

Third and Fourth
The Van Pool, 1942.

Messerschmitts: German fighter aircraft.

Irving: the Irving Air Chute company manufactured silk parachutes during World War II.

Haw-Haw: William Joyce, known as Lord Haw-Haw, was a fascist politician and Nazi propagandist. There were various wartime rumours that the Germans would attempt to poison the water supply.

pink limed cottages: in her diary entry for 6 March 1941, Roberts wrote 'this year Keidrych and I limed our cottage pink. Using for this process terracotta and a pleasing proportion of white lime.' *Diaries, Letters and Recollections*, p. 33.

Two golden-winged cupids: also mentioned in Rhys's poem 'Compassionate Leave' and Roberts's 'The Shadow Remains': 'And below, brazier fire that burns our sorrow,/ Dries weeping socks above on the rack: that knew/ Two angels pinned to the wall – again two'. Roberts, *Collected Poems*, p. 4.

Idyll on Active Service
The Van Pool, 1942.

Soldiers in Scapa
The Van Pool, 1942.

One of Rhys's military postings was to Scapa Flow, in Orkney.

Lament
The Van Pool, 1942.
In Memoriam T.J.M.C.: Timothy John Manley Corsellis (1921-41), poet, and leading aircraftsman in the Air Transport Auxiliary, who was killed when the plane he was piloting crashed near Dumfries on 10 October 1941. Rhys had included poems by Corsellis in both *Poems from the Forces* and *More Poems from the Forces*, the latter collection listing Corsellis 'In Memoriam', along with his close friend and fellow poet Nigel Weir, amongst others.

Swingfield near Hawkinge
The Van Pool, 1942.
Swingfield: the rural church of St Peter, at Swingfield, near to one of Rhys's wartime postings, has possible origins as early as the late 11th century. There is a simple war memorial, now commemorating the dead of both World Wars, attached to the lych-gate.

General Martel
The Van Pool, 1942; *More Poems from the Forces*, 1943.
General Martel: Sir Giffard Le Quesne Martel, 1889-1958, appointed Commander of the Royal Armoured Corps in 1940, and one of the leading experts in the development of tank warfare.

Fragment
The Van Pool, 1942.
Abelard: Pierre Abélard (1079-1142); French theologian and philosopher, infamously castrated as a result of his clandestine relationship with Héloïse, who was forced to retreat to a convent.
Burne-Jones: Edward Coley Burne-Jones (1833-98); Pre-Raphaelite artist.

Compassionate Leave: For Bruska
Kingdom Come, vol. 2, no. 3, Spring 1941, p. 84.
See also Roberts's 'The Shadow Remains', and Rhys's 'Third and Fourth' for other recurrences of the cupid motif. It is possible that Lynette Roberts's miscarriage in March 1940 is the initial context for this poem.
Bruska: A name taken and used by Roberts. Before she met Rhys, Roberts had trained in floristry under Constance Spry, and subsequently set up a flower business called 'Bruska'.
tear bottle: originally Roman, a small glass or other vessel for collecting tears in the process of mourning.

Tragic Guilt
Poetry: a Magazine of Verse, vol. 59, no. 4, 1942, p. 175; *Modern Welsh Poetry*, 1944.

Uncollected Poems

Tenement
Comment, vol. 2, no. 49, 28 November 1936, pp. 182-83.
This poem was published in the 'Poets' Corner' feature of *Comment*, edited

by Victor B. Neuburg. Neuburg (1883-1940) was an author, poet, and editor, and was instrumental in the early publication of Dylan Thomas, amongst others. He published an editorial comment underneath Rhys's poem: 'Impressionism in tragic jazz; a new development. This poet, by letting metre and rime run loose, gets right in with his theme; unconsciously proving an absolute sincerity. And note the close; it is, I think, perfect.'
Fabre: Jean-Henri Fabre, entomologist (1823-1915).

War-baby
Comment, vol. 3, no. 54, 2 January 1937, pp. 4-5.
This poem was also published in Neuburg's 'Poetry' competition section. His editorial comments on this poem are as follows: 'This frankly surrealist poem will irritate the literalists, Let it. This lyric is a flash-impression; that is, *an idea caught by subjective flashlight,* into which the time-element does not enter. The links are not sequent, but simultaneous. Only those who are "quick" or acute enough to take an impression as an impression will appreciate.'

Air Pageant
The Right Review, no. 2, February 1937, p. 13.
This edition of *The Right Review* was co-edited by Count Potocki of Montalk and Nigel Heseltine, the latter a friend of Rhys who was to take over the editing of *Wales* for numbers 8/9, 10 and 11 of the first series (August 1939, October 1939 and Winter 1939-40).

Building Job
Twentieth Century Verse, no. 3, April-May 1937, n.p

Rip Van Winkle
Twentieth Century Verse, no. 3, April-May 1937, n.p.
Rip Van Winkle: the eponymous farmer in a short story by Washington Irving who falls into a sleep for twenty years before returning to his home and inevitable change.
Rapunzel: from the tale by the brothers Grimm, the young girl kept trapped in a tower by a witch; she let down her long hair to provide a way for the witch, and subsequently, a prince, to visit her in the tower.

Wales on the Map
Life and Letters Today, vol. 16, no. 7, Spring-Summer 1937, pp. 45-46.
Bryan Elliff: Rhys's friend and correspondent Bryan Elliff appears to have provided him with London lodgings at various points in the 1930s.
pussmoth: name of a European moth, and an early 1930s monoplane built by de Havilland.
Bethlehem: the hamlet where Rhys was born.
gorsedd: the body of Celtic bards, especially now associated with the National Eisteddfod.
Sir Alfred Mond: Industrialist and politician (1868-1930), whose company 'Amalgamated Anthracite Collieries' dominated the Welsh anthracite industry.

sospanfach: 'little saucepan', a popular Welsh folksong.

spanish conscious: this poem was published in the course of the Spanish Civil War, and there was significant support from within Wales for the Republic and the International Brigades. See Robert Stradling, *Wales and the Spanish Civil War: the dragon's dearest cause?* (Cardiff: University of Wales Press, 2004).

Jubilee excursion: 1935 marked the Silver Jubilee of George V.

Cartoon Done in Something Will Be Done Week
Wales, no. 1, Summer 1937, pp. 25-27.

Moseley: perhaps Oswald Mosley, whose fascist political ambitions were significantly dented by the Cable Street riots of 1936.

Houston D.B.E: Dame Fanny Houston (1857-1936), described as an 'adventuress', Houston set up a rest home for frontline nurses during World War I, and was made DBE in 1917. See Richard Davenport-Hines, 'Houston, Dame Fanny Lucy (1857-1936)', *Oxford Dictionary of National Biography*, Oxford University Press, Sept 2004; online edn, Jan 2008 [http://www.oxforddnb.com/view/article/34015, accessed 8 Feb 2010].

slop: slang for 'policeman'.

Savage Club: a bohemian London gentleman's club particularly focused on the creative arts. Dylan Thomas was a member.

Litvinov: Maxim Litvinov (1876-1951), Soviet diplomat and commissar, responsible in the 1930s for the organisation of collective international resistance against Nazi Germany.

Mr. Baldwin has gone to the waters: Stanley Baldwin's final term as prime minister of the UK was 1935-37. In the middle of 1936 he suffered a period of exhaustion and enforced rest as a result in part of the increasing tensions relating to Hitler's remilitarisation of Germany and the International response to it.

Marx Webber: possibly a conflation of Karl Marx and Max Weber.

Intourist: founded in 1929 by Stalin, Intourist was the name of the official travel agency of the Soviet Union, which strove to provide a 'positive' experience of the Stalinist state for any Western visitors.

Finest Job: a military poster campaign ran with the slogan: 'The finest job in the world – work and play all over the globe'.

Black Watch: The Royal Highland Regiment of the British Army.

painopia: either a neologism or a mistranscription – perhaps of 'phanopoeia' (the poetic casting of images) if Rhys had been reading Ezra Pound's *ABC of Reading*, or of 'panoplia', a suit of armour.

tom-tom: a native East Indian drum.

King: Cecil Harmsworth King (1901-87), newspaper editor and publisher.

Novello: Ivor Novello (1893-1951), Welsh composer and actor. Later on, in 1960, Rhys had plans for a film entitled: 'The *Real* Ivor Novello Story'.

Menevia: Roman Catholic diocese in South Wales.

Socialites
Wales, no. 1, Summer 1937, p. 27.

The Fire Sermon or Bureaucracy Burned
Wales, no. 2, August 1937, p. 69.
Penrhos Aerodrome: The poem describes an incendiary nationalist protest headed by Saunders Lewis: 'In 1936 Lewis made a dramatic political challenge to his fellow countrymen which became a landmark in modern Welsh history and in the history of Welsh letters in the twentieth century. The Air Ministry acceded to objections by naturalists in England to the setting up of a bombing range in East Anglia and chose instead a location in the heartland of Welsh language and culture, Penyberth on the Llŷn peninsula in north-west Wales. The vast majority of Welsh public opinion vehemently opposed the proposal, but to no avail. Lewis decided to take direct action, and on the fourth centenary of the Act of Union, to challenge the constitutional legality of England to over-rule the wishes of the Welsh. Together with prominent Baptist minister Lewis Valentine, and teacher and short-story writer D.J. Williams, he set fire to the bombing school and then gave himself up to the police. The three were tried at Caernarfon assizes for the arson attack – where Lewis made a speech described by A J.P. Taylor as reaching rare heights of noble oratory. The jury failed to agree, and the trial was moved to the Old Bailey, where the three were sentenced to nine months' imprisonment.' Harri Pritchard-Jones, 'Lewis, (John) Saunders (1893-1985)', *Oxford Dictionary of National Biography*, Oxford University Press, Sept 2004; online edn, Oct 2008 [http://www.oxforddnb.com/view/article/55454, accessed 25 March 2010]. See M. Wynn Thomas for a brief evaluation of this poem, and Rhys's inclusion of a poem on the same subject by Gwenallt in a subsequent edition of *Wales* (*Corresponding Cultures: the two literatures of Wales* (Cardiff: University of Wales Press, 1999), pp. 84-85).
Taliesin: Sixth-century Celtic poet, some of whose work survives through medieval manuscript (The 'Book of Taliesin').

Cross Country
Life and Letters Today, vol. 17, no. 9, Autumn 1937, p. 82.
carded makes: in the 1930s aviation cigarette cards were popular amongst schoolboy collectors.
Woodbines: a make of strong cigarettes popular with the armed forces.
L.A.C.: Leading Aircraftsmen.

Special Area
Life and Letters Today, vol. 17, no. 9, Autumn 1937, p. 83.
The Special Areas (Development and Improvement) Act 1934 specified areas, including South Wales, that required particular economic assistance.

Spilling the Beans
Life and Letters Today, vol. 17, no. 9, Autumn 1937, p. 83.
Diawl: devil.
Lord Melchett: the title taken by Sir Alfred Mond on entering the House of Lords. See note to 'Wales on the Map'.
Jeremy Taylor: scholar, author and cleric (c. 1613-67). In the mid 1640s

Taylor was living and working in Carmarthenshire.

Youth
Life and Letters Today, vol. 17, no. 10, Winter 1937, p. 67; *Modern Welsh Poetry*, 1944.

Cynghanedd Cymry
Transition, no. 26, 1937, pp.173-74.
Cynghanedd Cymry: Rhys was later to comment in an editorial: 'and the facsimile of the master's [James Joyce's] handwriting reproduced opposite the preface, which is by B.J. Morse, drove my nostalgic mind back to a most interesting letter (since regretfully lost by a girl on its way to the National Library) that I had received from him upon the publication of one of my early poems in *Transition* in 1937, in which big chunks of "Work in Progress" appeared serially. I still like to flatter myself that Joyce's references to *cynghanedd, englynion*, and the River Towy in Finnegan's [sic] Wake were due to that early non-Cymric piece of experimentation of mine, but this presumption no doubt is quite unfounded conceit on my part.' *Wales*, vol. 4, no. 6, Winter 1944-45, pp. 7-8.

Landmark
Twentieth Century Verse, no. 8, January-February 1938, n.p.

During Lambing Season
Twentieth Century Verse, no. 10, May 1938, p.40, with title: 'Triads During Lambing Season'; *Modern Welsh Poetry*, 1944.
Triad: (Welsh *Trioedd*) a traditional formal organisation originating in Welsh language medieval poetry.
Talley: village near Bethlehem in Carmarthenshire.
Mothvey: English transliteration of Myddfai, a village to the north east of Llangadog.
Goldengrove: the Estate Gelli Aur, again, local to Rhys's home area of Carmarthenshire.

The Last Supper
Twentieth Century Verse, no. 10, May 1938, p. 40.

Tri Englyn
Right Review, no. 6, July 1938, p. 8.
Englyn: a traditional Welsh language short poem form. Rhys adapts to his own purposes some aspects of the variety of prescribed forms, such as the use of internal rhyme, consonantal patterning, and four-line stanzas.
Breton fisherfolk: Rhys is speculating on the subject of common Celtic ancestries.
Stockbreeder: probably the journal *Farmer and Stockbreeder*, highly influential in farming and agricultural communities at the time.
Bolshevia: occasionally used to denote the Soviet Union, but here perhaps a play on Menevia, the Welsh Roman Catholic diocese.
Old Llewelyn: legend has it that Llywelyn ap Gruffydd, thirteenth-century Prince and last 'independent' ruler of Wales, tried to escape his English

pursuers by reversing his horse's shoes. However, betrayed by the blacksmith, he was caught and beheaded at Cefn y Bedd. Another strand of the legend includes an illicit liaison with a 'sportive girl'.

Fragments from the Poem of Asking
Life and Letters Today, vol. 18, no. 12, Summer 1938, pp. 52-53.
SOSPAN FACH: lines from the popular Welsh song, roughly translated as: 'the little saucepan boils on the fire, the big saucepan boils over the floor, the cat is scratching little Johnny on the cheek'.

Tryst
Seven, no. 1, Summer 1938, p. 36.

Black Trust
Partisan Review, vol. 6, no. 1, Fall 1938, p. 92. Published in a section within the *Review* entitled 'A Little Anthology of British Poets', edited by D.S. Savage.

Understood by Boadicea and King Arthur
The Voice of Scotland, vol. 1, no. 3, December 1938-February 1939, p. 8.
D.S. Savage: poet and author (1917-2007). Savage was contributing poems to many of the same little magazines as Rhys throughout the late 1930s, and selected Rhys's poem 'Black Trust' for his 'A Little Anthology of British Poets' published in the *Partisan Review* (Fall 1938).

Nonconformity
Poetry: A Magazine of Verse, vol. 53, no. 4, January 1939, pp. 186-87.

Treasury
Poetry: A Magazine of Verse, vol. 53, no. 4, January 1939, pp. 187-89.

Landscape Piece
The Listener, vol. 21, no. 526, 9 February 1939, p. 300; *The Phoenix*, vol. 2, no. 2, September 1939, p. 85.

Homage to a Split Man
Poetry London, no. 1, February 1939, n.p.
At one point this poem had an alternative possible title of 'Homage to a Jekyll and Hyde'. It is inspired by the biographical subject of 'Peter Warlock', the pseudonym of Philip Heseltine (1894-1930), Anglo-Welsh composer and father of Rhys's friend Nigel Heseltine. Philip Heseltine studied at Eton, in Cologne, and at Oxford. An infamous drinker and supposed occultist, he inspired literary characters in fiction by Osbert Sitwell, D.H. Lawrence, and Aldous Huxley, amongst others. He died of coal gas poisoning.
Jenny Lind: Swedish opera star (1820-87).

Ephemerae for Bruska
Wales, no. 6/7, March 1939, p. 201; *Modern Welsh Poetry*, 1944.
Bruska: a name used by Lynette Roberts, both for herself and her flower selling business.
taught a bird the word: presumably a reference to Branwen, in *The Mabinogion*, who teaches a starling to speak in order to send a message to

her brother, Bran, King of Britain.
Arthur's hound: in the tale of 'Culhwch and Olwen' in *The Mabinogion*, Arthur's dog Cafall kills Ysgithyrwyn Chief Boar.
the physicians: another oblique reference to the tale of Llyn y Fan Fach and the physicians of Myddfai.
three-breasted lover: in Celtic mythology, Gwen Teirbron.

Sheep
Life and Letters Today, vol. 21, no. 21, May 1939, pp. 58-59; *Modern Welsh Poetry*, 1944.
Cheviots: a kind of white-faced hill sheep.

Coracle
The Welsh Review, vol. 1, no. 6, July 1939, p. 314.
licensed waterman: commercial coracle fishing is a licensed trade.

Spell
Life and Letters Today, vol. 22, no. 23, July 1939, pp. 57-58.
Noson Lawen: a traditional Welsh musical gathering, usually in the evening.
Sêt Fawr: the 'big seat' in chapel where the chapel elders were allowed to sit, therefore associated with (oppressive) moral authority.

Death-dance or Case History of the Lustrous Navel
Wales, no. 10, October 1939, p. 270.
Sparkenbroke: Sparkenbroke is the eponymous hero of the Anglo-Welsh novelist Charles Morgan's popular 1936 novel, a tale of art, frustrated love, death and attempted suicide. See Etienne Gilson: 'It has been said of Sparkenbroke that he was Byron and Shelley in one. Undoubtedly, but he is also Wagner, Charles Morgan and, broadly speaking, any artist who is conscious of the intimate relationship existing between art, love and death.' *Dante and Philosophy* (New York and London: Harper Row, 1963), p. 287.

The Van Pool
Wales, no. 10, October 1939, p. 271.

Laugharne Pastoral
Wales, no. 10, October 1939, pp. 274-75.

'Shift'
Life and Letters Today, vol. 23, no. 27, November 1939, p. 197.
A typescript of this poem carries the title 'Migration', crossed through and replaced with 'Mutation'.

Poem
Fantasy: A Literary Quarterly, no. 3, 1939, p.14.

The Van Pool: Tichrig
Wales, no. 11, Winter 1939-40, pp. 292-93. Also published under the title 'Trichrug, North Carmarthen' in *Seven*, vol. 6, no. 3 [1947], pp. 60-61.
In a letter to Rhys dated 17 May 1946, Sydney Tremayne, the editor of *Seven* wrote: 'Of these I like best Trichrig [sic], but the typescript is in such a state that I can't guarantee I'm reading it properly. Perhaps you could let me have

another copy before we inflict it on the printer... I like the sharp, clear-cut images and find the atmosphere most effective. Would £2-2 be a satisfactory rate?' (Source: ms letter, Stanley Lewis papers).

Tichrig: Trichrug in Carmarthenshire (here variously spelt), is the 400-metre-high hill that lies south east of the hamlet of Bethlehem behind Garn Goch.

Llansadwrn: opposite in the sense of being the other side of the river Tywi in the valley.

Garn Goch: see the poem 'Garn Goch' and its associated note.

leet courts: localised courts overseeing the jurisdiction of the Lord of the Manor.

homagers: manorial tenants.

Landskip: landscape (often, in painting).

Eirlys: see note to 'The Prodigal Speaks'.

River Sawdde
Life and Letters Today, vol. 24, no. 31, March 1940, p. 278 (with the title 'Sawdde'); *Modern Welsh Poetry*, 1944.

Sawdde: the river Sawdde runs close to Bethlehem.

'twmpath': mound on a village green; traditionally the focal point of communal dancing and music.

Song
Now [Series 1], no. 1, Easter 1940, p. 5.

G.P. bombs: General Purpose bombs.

Vickers: manufacturer of munitions and aircraft, amongst other things.

'Scorpiones Pungunt': the Latin motto of No. 84 Squadron RAF, meaning 'scorpions sting'.

Phosgene and thermite: Phosgene gas was used as a chemical weapon during World War I, and stockpiled during World War II; thermite is a substance used in incendiary bombs and other military applications.

Rumour round the Farmyard
Now [Series 1], no. 1, Easter 1940, p. 6.

gambos: gambo is a term used for a farm cart in South Wales.

Welsh Song
Furioso, vol. 1, no. 3, Spring 1940, p. 30.

A White Lady and a tail-less sow: in Welsh legend 'y Ladi Wen' and 'Hwch Ddu Gwta' are spirits associated with Halloween.

Fame
Kingdom Come, vol. 2, no. 1, Autumn 1940, p. 27.

Vans: Carmarthenshire mountains.

Stapledon: Sir George Stapledon (1882-1960) was an eminent and influential Professor of Agriculture at Aberystwyth.

Lindberg: possibly Charles Lindbergh, who in the early 1940s campaigned to keep the United States out of World War II.

Chessman Associations

Now [Series 1], no. 3, 1940, p. 5; *Little Reviews Anthology*, 1943.
There is a manuscript version of this poem in the National Library of Wales archive with the title: 'Father Figures'.
Shelley: Percy Bysshe Shelley had various connections to Wales, and in 1812-13 was living at Tan-yr-allt in Tremadog.
Wordsworth: in late summer 1824 William Wordsworth made a tour of Wales, in which he encountered the 'Ladies of Llangollen', Lady Eleanor Butler and the Hon. Sarah Ponsonby, at their Dee-side home, and visited the Devil's Bridge. See his sonnets 'To the Lady E.B. and the Hon. Miss P.' and 'The Devil's Bridge, North Wales'.
Charleville: Arthur Rimbaud was born in the French town of Charleville.
Landor: Walter Savage Landor (1775-1864), poet and author, invested much of his family inheritance into the attempted development of the Llanthony estate in the Black Mountains.

Cinque Ports
Life and Letters Today, vol. 28, January-March 1941, pp. 238-39; *Poems from the Forces*, 1941.
Dunsany's latest alarm: the author Lord Dunsany (1878-1957). 'At the outbreak of World War II he [Dunsany] joined the Local Defence Volunteers (the Home Guard), watching for incoming German airplanes from Dunstall Priory.' S.T. Joshi, *Lord Dunsany: master of the Anglo-Irish imagination* (Westport, CT: Greenwood Press, 1995), p. 8.
Blenheims: British light bomber aircraft, active in the early 1940s.
Empson's villanelle: William Empson's poem was first published in the *Cambridge Review* in 1928.
Dornier 17: German light bomber aircraft.
'ubique quo fas et gloria ducunt': from the Monogram of the Royal Engineers, meaning 'Everywhere where right and glory lead'.
Lotus ad: a 1941 advertising campaign by Lotus shoes coincided with the introduction of clothes rationing.

Manly and Elizabethan
Kingdom Come, vol. 2, no. 3, Spring 1941, p. 96.

Ridiculous Wrench
Now [Series 1], no. 7, 1941, p. 25.
Ruthven: Ruthven Todd (1914-78), poet and novelist. Possibly a reference to Todd's poem 'In September, 1937'.

Poem to Bill Empson
Poems from the Forces, 1941.
Rhys was reading William Empson at this time (see note to 'Cinque Ports').
Empson's poem 'Ignorance of Death' was published in his collection *The Gathering Storm* (1940).

The Fox
The Listener, vol. 28, no. 719, 22 October 1942, p. 526; *London Welshman*, vol. 16, no. 9, September 1961, p.11.

Translated from the Welsh 'Y Llwynog' by R. Williams Parry.
A manuscript of this translation is in the Stanley Lewis papers.

Sheep: Gwynfe
Poetry London, vol. 2, no. 7, October-November 1942, pp. 35-36.
Gwynfe: a small Carmarthenshire settlement not far from Bethlehem. Rhys also entitled an autobiographical poem 'Gwynfe', which exists in incomplete manuscript in the National Library of Wales archive.
cheviots: breed of sheep.

The Cock Pheasant
The Listener, vol. 28, no. 725, 3 December 1942, p. 711; *London Welshman*, vol. 16, no. 7, July 1961, p. 13.
Translated from the Welsh 'Y Ceiliog Ffesant' by R. Williams Parry.

Trimming Hedges
Poetry Folios, no. 2, Winter 1942-43, n.p.
Adlestrop: near Oxford. See the English pastoral poem by Edward Thomas.
Grantchester: near Cambridge. See Rupert Brooke's pastoral poem 'The Old Vicarage, Grantchester': 'Unkempt about those hedges blows/ An unofficial English rose'.
Cae Fair: 'Mary's Field.'

The Life of Man
Life and Letters Today, vol. 36, January-March 1943, p. 178.
Y Ficer Rhys Prichard: 'the vicar' Rhys Prichard, clergyman and poet, born at Llandovery in Carmarthenshire. His collected poems on religious themes became known under the title *Canwyll y Cymry* ('The Welshmen's Candle').

In Memoriam
The Listener, vol. 29, no. 735, 11 February 1943, p. 180.
The Welsh language poet R. Williams Parry (1884-1956) wrote many short strict-metre poems (englynion) in memory of those who died during the First World War.
Rhys here translates from the Welsh of R. Williams Parry's 'Milwr' and 'Morwr'. See also note to 'War Memorial', 'His Father's Son' and 'Soldier from Merioneth.

Death of a Hurricane Pilot
Poetry Folios, no. 3, Summer 1943; *More Poems from the Forces*, 1943; *New Road*, 1944.
On 1 November 1940, Roger de Cannart d'Hamale, a 21-year old Belgian Hurricane fighter pilot flying with RAF No. 46 Squadron, was shot down at 22,000 feet, crashing at Smersole Farm off the Canterbury Road near Dover.
Buffs and Green Howards: regiments of the British Army.
Tiger Gort: John Standish Surtees Prendergast Vereker, sixth Viscount Gort, attended Sandhurst Royal Military College 1905-06, and was Commander in the field of the British Army 1940-41.
'Cassandra' of the *Mirror*: pen name of journalist Sir William Neil Connor, writing for Cecil King's *Daily Mirror*. He was variously critical of the way in

which the government conducted the war. In his 'Introduction' to *Poems from the Forces* Rhys mentions 'Cassandra' as one of the few journalists prepared to publicize advance notices of the anthology.

Llangadog Common
Wales, vol. 3, no. 2, October-December 1943, p. 35.
In manuscript this poem was initially titled 'Carmarthen Farm'.

Stone
Wales, vol. 3, no. 2, October-December 1943, p. 35.
memorial to a famous warhorse: it is possible that Rhys has partly in mind Captain Godfrey Morgan, Lord Tredegar, who erected a monument to his horse 'Sir Briggs' at Tredegar House near Newport. Both horse and rider had earlier survived the Charge of the Light Brigade during the Crimean War.

Flashbacks
Wales, vol. 3, no. 2, October-December 1943, p. 36.

Air Raid on East Coast
Bugle Blast: An Anthology from the Services, ed. Jack Aistrop and Reginald Moore (London: George Allen and Unwin, 1943), pp. 104-07.
Dornier 215: German aircraft used as a night fighter and light bomber.
traversed: to alter the position of an anti-aircraft gun laterally in taking aim.
instrument numbers: employed to take height measurements of incoming aircraft.
Heinkel: another make of German aircraft.
19-year-old M.M.: Military Medal. Cf. 'Alarm Alarm'.

48 hours at Tenby
More Poems from the Forces, 1943.
Caldy: (Ynys Bŷr) a holy island south of Tenby, home to a monastery.
St Catherine's Island: (Ynys Catrin) is home to a nineteenth-century fort.
Herbert M. Vaughan: (1870-1948) author of *The South Wales Squires* (1926).

Alarm, Alarm
More Poems from the Forces, 1943; *New Road*, 1944; *A New Romantic Anthology*, ed. Stefan Schimanski and Henry Treece (London: Grey Walls Press, 1949), p. 179.
monument to the builder of the Japanese navy: a reference to William Adams (1564-1620), reputedly the first Englishman to reach Japan in 1600, where he became advisor to the shogun, and assisted in the construction of ships. Forbidden to leave Japan, he died there a prosperous and powerful man. A monument to Adams was unveiled in Gillingham in 1934.
Detling, Hawkinge: Rhys was stationed in Kent in 1940, and lists the various Kentish locations of his wartime experience in the Royal Artillery.
M.M.: Military Medal. Cf. 'Air Raid on East Coast'.
Martlesham Heath: RAF base near Ipswich. Rhys was briefly stationed at Gorleston on Sea, Great Yarmouth.
Italian raid: in November 1940 Italian aircraft made their only attack on the

Thames Estuary.

South Ronaldsay: Rhys was also stationed in the Orkney Islands in 1941 where he formed part of the defensive anti-aircraft batteries defending the Home Fleet, which was based in Scapa Flow.

The Prince of Wales: battleship HMS *Prince of Wales* was fully commissioned in March 1941. Rhys may well have sighted the ship carrying Churchill to the Newfoundland conference in August 1941. HMS *Prince of Wales* was sunk off the coast of Malaya in December 1941 by the Japanese. Rhys no doubt intends the historical ironies with reference to William Adams.

OSDEF: Orkney and Shetland Defences.

Digging planes: see 'Death of a Hurricane Pilot'.

King's Bench Walk The 'Temple' burning: Lynette Roberts was later to recall: 'I missed Keidrych dreadfully. I joined him in Yarmouth and had to pass through London so I went to Celia Buckmaster's home at Kings Bench Walk. I was astonished to find the results of a raid were still pending after days.' *Diaries, Letters and Recollections*, p. 218. See also *Diaries, Letters and Recollections*, p. 46, and Roberts's poem 'Crossed and Uncrossed':

> Still water silences death: fills night with curious light,
> Brings green peace and birds to top of Plane tree
> Fills Magnolia with grail thoughts: while you of King's Bench
> Walk, cherish those you most love. (*Collected Poems*, p. 21).

Room with a View

Poetry Quarterly, vol. 6, no. 1, Spring 1944, p. 9.

bootless cries: see Shakespeare, 'Sonnet 29': 'And trouble deaf heaven with my bootless cries'.

triads: see note to 'Triads During Lambing Season'.

Castle: Llansteffan is famous, inter alia, for its Norman castle, captured in 1146 by the Prince Rhys ap Gruffydd, and for its sandy beaches. It is the village where Rhys and Roberts got married, and it is only two miles from Llanybri.

War Memorial; His Father's Son; Soldier from Merioneth

Wales, vol. 3, no. 4, Summer 1944, p. 33.

These poems are further translations from the Welsh of R. Williams Parry. 'War Memorial' is a translation of 'Ar Gofadail', 'His Father's Son' is a translation of 'Mab ei Dad' which was written in memory of Llewelyn ap Tomos Shankland who died on 25 November 1917. 'Soldier from Merioneth' is a translation of 'Milwr o Feirion', which was written in memory of Thomas Jones of Cwm Main, Penllyn who died on 27 August 1916. See also the note to 'In Memoriam'.

Incorruptible

Wales, vol. 3, no. 4, Summer 1944, p. 33.

D. Gwenallt Jones: Welsh language poet (1899-1968).

The Soldier's Plaint

Poetry Scotland, no. 1, 1944, p. 38.

tozing: usually, to describe the separation of fibres in the combing of wool; teasing.

Poem of Asking
Poetry Scotland, no. 1, 1944, p. 39.
James Findlay Hendry: Scottish poet and editor (1912-86), who edited the influential anthology *The New Apocalypse* (1939). Rhys included some of Hendry's poems in both *Poems from the Forces* and *More Poems from the Forces*. In 1938 Rhys was presumably staying with Hendry as various items of Rhys's correspondence were addressed c/o Hendry, 20 Vernon Road, Leeds. See Dylan Thomas, *The Collected Letters*, ed. Paul Ferris (London: J.M. Dent, 2000), p. 349.

The Curlew
Wales, vol. 5, no. 7, Summer 1945, p. 18.
A translation of 'Y Gylfinir' by R. Williams Parry.

A Sailor's Epitaph
Wales, vol. 5, no. 7, Summer 1945, p. 20.
Tudno: Thomas Tudno Jones, cleric and Welsh language poet (1844-1895).

Solitude and The Stone
Wales, vol. 5, no. 7, Summer 1945, p. 21.
penillion: traditional Welsh language verse form, often for musical accompaniment.

Inscription for a Girl's Grave
Wales, vol. 5, no. 7, Summer 1945, p.21.

Englyn: Snowdonia
Wales, vol. 5, no. 7, Summer 1945, p.21.

Gwilym Cowlyd: Welsh poet (1828-1904).

The Battle of the Cambrians and the Mice
Wales, vol. 5, nos. 8/9, December 1945, p. 82.
In 1709 Edward Holdsworth published a satirical mock-epic poem, in Latin, entitled *Cambromyomachia*, which translates as 'the battle of the Cambrians (Welsh) and the mice'. The poem was variously translated into English in the years following, with titles such as 'Muscipula' and 'The Mouse-trap'. It is a tale of a Welsh plague of cheese-eating mice, and of the invention of a trap by a cunning smith called Taffy, who entices the mouse into a cage with a morsel of toasted cheese. The trapped mouse is then handed to the cat, which plays with it and then kills it, so reintroducing a plentiful supply of food once more. Whilst the satire is of the gentlest comic kind, there is comparison made between the mouse's usual defence from the cat of taking refuge in a space too small for the cat to follow, and the way in which the Welsh held off Julius Caesar by retreating to refuges too small too conquer and too difficult to access.
cui Wallia numquam aequalem peperit: 'whose equal had not been seen in Wales before'.

Secular Mystique
Wales, vol. 5, nos. 8/9, December 1945, p. 81.

Dog
Wales, vol. 5, nos. 8/9, December 1945, p. 82.

Poem on Being Invalided Out of the Army
Now [Series 2], vol. 5, 1945, p. 39.
Robert Hewison asserts that Rhys was among a number of writers who were treated at the Northfield Military Hospital in the suburbs of south Birmingham. This was a forward-looking psychiatric hospital that pioneered therapeutic treatment. See Robert Hewison, *Under Siege: Literary Life in London 1939-45* (London: Methuen, 1988), p. 70.

First Peace Christmas
Life and Letters, vol. 52, January-March 1947, p. 176.
Alun Llywelyn-Williams: poet (1913-88), born in Cardiff.

Epitaph
Wales, vol. 8, no. 29, May 1948, p. 531.
Rhys's early notebook contains a manuscript of this poem.
faery Lady: once again, Rhys draws on the legend of the 'Van Pool'.

Proem
Wales, vol. 8, no. 29, May 1948, p. 532.
Robert Herring: (1903-75) poet and editor of *Life and Letters Today*.

For the Late Lord Howard de Walden
Wales, vol. 8, no. 29, May 1948, p. 532.
Lord Howard de Walden: Thomas Evelyn Scott-Ellis (1880-1946); aristocrat, author and patron of the arts. Howard de Walden had many Welsh interests, and contributed an essay entitled 'Towards a Welsh Theatre' to *Wales*, vol. 3, no. 4, Summer 1944, pp. 8-12. He wrote the libretti for an operatic trilogy inspired by *The Mabinogion*, entitled *The Cauldron of Annwn* (music by Joseph Holbrooke).
Chirk: Howard de Walden's home was Chirk Castle, Denbighshire.
Ceiriog: a valley in what was Denbighshire.

Ministry of Information: Malet Street
Wales, vol. 8, no. 29, May 1948, p. 533.
Malet Street: the University of London's Senate House was used as the home of the Ministry of Information during World War II. Rhys worked for the Ministry in the later stages of the war.
Cecil Day Lewis: from 1941 the poet Cecil Day-Lewis (1904-72) worked as an editor in the Ministry of Information's publications division.

Literary 'Conservatives'
Wales, vol. 8, no. 29, May 1948, p. 533.

On Reading Certain 'Anglo–Welsh' Literary Criticism
Wales, vol. 8, no. 29, May 1948, p. 533.
In manuscript the title of the poem continues: 'by a Mr E. Glyn Lewis'

(Stanley Lewis papers).

Shoni-Hoi: a figure from Welsh folklore who manipulated the weather to the benefit of smugglers and wreckers.

Bardic Crown Ballad

Wales, vol. 8, no. 29, May 1948, pp. 538-39.

Schmeisser: an Ally name for a German MP40 submachine gun.

sent our dispatches off home: later in the war, Rhys was working for the Ministry of Information.

Reichswald: the battle of Reichswald took place in February and March 1945, resulting in heavy casualties.

Victoria Leave Train

Wales, vol. 8, no. 29, May 1948, pp. 539-40.

booby-trapped dead: there were rumours and accounts that German troops booby-trapped the bodies of dead soldiers during the Normandy landings.

Aberfan: Under the Arc Lights

Spectator, 28 October 1966, p. 554; *Best Poems of 1966*.

144 people were killed in the Aberfan disaster on 21 October 1966.

Ceridwen: in Welsh legend, the enchantress Ceridwen and her cauldron gave rise to the birth/transformation of Taliesin, the famous Welsh bard.

world-shared audience in their evening room: in the same edition of the *Spectator* Stuart Hood wrote a television review of the coverage of the disaster: 'The first question is: Were the television organisations right in providing live coverage of the Aberfan disaster? The answer is unequivocally 'Yes'...There was no more accurate or poignant method of reporting the tragedy than to let us see the faces of the men and women waiting as the rescuers dug into the black mud.' *Spectator*, 28 October 1966, p. 541.

Uncollected and Unpublished Poems

On Remand

Stanley Lewis papers.

The poem's note, place and date [2222 Brixton 1936] suggest that it was inspired by Rhys's own prosecution. See Introduction for details.

Conversation in the Black-Maria

Stanley Lewis papers.

Stablelamp and Bedding

Stanley Lewis papers.

Milk Bars: the Milk Marketing Board promoted retail milk bars to increase consumer consumption of milk from 1935 onwards. See Derek J. Oddy: 'By the end of 1935 there were twenty-seven milk bars open in Britain, 587 by the end of 1936 and 1,010 by the end of 1937.' *From Plain Fare to Fusion: British Diet from the 1890s to the 1990s* (Woodbridge: Boydell Press, 2003), p. 109.

C.W.S.: the Co-operative Wholesale Society.

Foreign News
Stanley Lewis papers.
Tercet and a Lyric Interlude
Houghton Library Archive, Harvard University, bMS Am 1641.1 (23).
Hanes gwaed ifanc y tywydd
Houghton Library Archive, Harvard University, bMS Am 1641.1 (17).
Hanes gwaed ifanc y tywydd: in translation 'the history of the young blood of the weather'.
The phrases in Welsh within the poem are all proverbial.
Gorau cam, cam cyntaf: 'the best step is the first step'.
the red red garn: evocative of Garn Goch, near Bethlehem.
Cas gŵr na châr ei wlad : 'hateful is the man who does not love his country'.
Gwell pwyll nag aur: 'better wisdom than gold'.
Nid ar drot y mae cardota chwaith: 'you cannot beg in haste either'.
Dyfal donc a dyrr y garreg : 'the persistent tap breaks the stone'.
Nid tân, heb eirias: 'there is no such thing as a fire without a flame blazing'.

Violence: Wales: 63-64
National Library of Wales Archive, NLW MS 23427E.
In 1963 there were plans to drown the valley of the village of Llangyndeyrn, Carmarthenshire, by damming the Gwendraeth Fach to create a reservoir to provide water supply to Swansea. There was a successful resistance campaign, fought in the context of growing protest at the creation of a dam in the Tryweryn valley (see note to part II of this poem). However, the Gwendraeth Fach project was merely displaced to a different location, culminating in the damming of the river Tywi, and the opening of the Llyn Brianne scheme, near Llandovery, in 1973.
Llangendeirne: properly, Llangyndeyrn.
Rhandirmwyn: village near Llandovery, close to Llyn Brianne.
highwayman's uninhabited cave: a manuscript notation on the typescript makes it clear that Rhys is referring to Twm Sion Cati, infamous sixteenth-century highwayman, whose cave hideaway is located on the slopes of Dinas Hill near Rhandirmwyn.
Gwendraeth Fach: the branch of the river, eventually flowing into the Tywi estuary, on which is situated Llangyndeyrn.
Shir Gâr: popular form of Sir Gaerfyrddin, the Welsh language name for Carmarthenshire.
Ruddy-deaf-aid: one of the annotated typescripts makes it clear that Rhys is punning on 'Rhyd-y-Defaid', the name of a mining area in the Clyne Valley near Swansea, in a region that was developed for residential housing during the 1950s.
hwyl: a complex word in Welsh, perhaps here with the sense of 'religious fervour'.
cawl: traditional Welsh soup.
Llangefni: Henry Brooke, the then Minister for Welsh Affairs, had planned

to speak at the 1957 National Eisteddfod in Llangefni, but he pulled out owing to growing unrest over the plans to flood the Tryweryn valley in order to create a reservoir to supply the city of Liverpool with water, destroying a community and Capel Celyn in the process. The railroading of these plans through British Parliament led to increasing political and direct-action protests from 1963 onwards, including the setting of an explosive charge at an electricity transformer on the building site of the dam in February 1963. In 1969 Gwynfor Evans wrote in a letter to *The Times*: 'There has been some violence in Wales. It started after the Government has shown its contempt for the remarkably united and powerful but wholly constitutional opposition to the drowning of Cwm Tryweryn and the destruction of the fine Welsh-speaking community which lived there. Some young men felt in 1962 that they were "left with no alternative" and so had to resort to other means.' ('Letters to the Editor', *The Times*, 28 April 1969, p. 9.).

Bosworth: at the Battle of Bosworth Field the Welsh-descended Henry Tudor defeated Richard III to become King Henry VII.

Tonypandy riots: industrial mining conflict occasioning violence between capital and labour in the Rhondda in 1910-11, in which workers' protests were met with the disproportionate responses of the British government, but from which a new perspective on the collective power of unionised labour was to emerge.

Index of First Lines